WHAT'S ON YOUR MIND?

MERLIN R. CAROTHERS

Unless otherwise identified, all Scripture references are taken from the King James Version of the Bible.

Scripture quotations identified TLB are from *The Living Bible Paraphrased* (Wheaton: Tyndale house Publishers, 1971)

Scripture quotations identified NAS are from *The New American Standard Bible*, copyright 1960, 1975 by the Lockman Foundation.

Scripture quotations identified PHILLIPS are from *The New Testament in Modern English*, copyright 1958, 1972 by J.B. Phillips.

Scripture quotations identified RSV are from *The Revised Standard*, copyright 1962 by The World Publishing Company.

Scripture quotations identified GN are from *Good News For Modern Man*, copyright 1966, 1971 by the American Bible Society.

Scripture quotations identified AMP are from the *Amplified New Testament*, copyright 1958 by the Lockman Foundation.

Scripture quotations identified MLB are from the *Modern Language Bible*, copyright 1945, 1969 by the Zondervan Publishing House.

Scripture quotations identified TLB are from *The Living Bible Paraphrased* (Wheaton: Tyndale House Publishers, 1971)

WHAT'S ON YOUR MIND?
ISBN 0-943026-13-X
Copyright 1984 by Merlin R. Carothers
All rights reserved
Printed in the United States of America
Published by Merlin R. Carothers, Escondido, California

CONTENTS

Other Best-Selling Books
by
MERLIN R. CAROTHERS
Prison to Praise
Power in Praise
Answers to Praise
Praise Works
Walking and Leaping
Bringing Heaven into Hell
Victory on Praise Mountain
The Bible on Praise
More Power to You!

Books by Merlin Carothers have had such dramatic impact upon their readers that they have been translated, printed and distributed in more languages than any other contemporary Christian book.

PREFACE

Imagine a motion-picture screen above your head. Now visualize on that screen the thoughts that have come to your mind in recent weeks. Would you be ashamed for everyone you know to see your thoughts? If so, you urgently need to read and understand, "What's on Your Mind?" I wish I had known these truths when I was a young man.

I will share with you what I have learned, and I pray that God will take these words and use them to spare *you* needless suffering.

I'm writing this book because I need to read it, because God is burning it into my own heart — constraining me to make it available to others.

PLEASE CONSIDER THE FOLLOWING QUESTION: WHICH ARE MORE IMPORTANT TO GOD?

1. Our Actions

2. Our thoughts and desires

Wait until you have read this book before answering.

INTRODUCTION

I was sure it could never happen.

I was positive it couldn't happen.

I knew, without a doubt, it was impossible for it to happen.

IT HAPPENED.

My desires changed! I no longer *wanted* to think immoral thoughts.

A miracle? No, a discovery!

For the first time in my life I would be pleased for my wife to know everything in my thoughts. It would not embarrass me for my daughters to know all the thoughts of my heart. I could look at any woman, even the most beautiful, and feel free to reveal to her everything that was in my mind.

God had sent me on a journey that would change the most secret parts of my thoughts and desires...

CHAPTER ONE
A MINISTER FALLS

The minister sat across from me, tears streaming down his face as if he had lost everything in the world that was important to him. And indeed he was very close to losing everything that he had taken a lifetime to build. A lifetime of sacrifice, hard work and helping others was about to be shattered. This is the story he told me.

His secretary had made an appointment for him to counsel the most attractive lady in their congregation. He was pleased that she was coming. Wherever she went, men always stopped to give her admiring glances that nearly always turned into prolonged stares. It was obvious that she was aware of the attention and that she thoroughly enjoyed it. But as far as the pastor knew, she was not interested in a close relationship with any man.

The pastor explained that when the woman came into his office he experienced a sense of physical pleasure. He had always considered himself happily-married and had carefully protected himself from ever doing anything that would taint his image as a "Man of God". He and his wife were raising several children in what he considered an exceptionally happy home. Members of the congregation often referred to them as the "ideal family".

The woman's problem was quite unusual. She lived with

a continual feeling of guilt because of her constant desire to have sex with different men. Her appetite for immorality haunted her day and night. She explained a few details of her lurid past, but assured him that since becoming a Christian several years earlier, she had been able to control her passions — until now.

The crisis point in the counseling session came when she told him that more than anything in all the world she wanted to have a physical relationship with him, her pastor. Instead of cutting her off at this point, he sat and listened as she explained in detail everything that she would like to do with him.

The pastor told me that it required all the strength he could muster to usher the woman out of his office.

For several weeks all he could do was think about this woman. He repeatedly told himself that if she were scheduled to see him again, he would make sure that his wife was present. But she came back to the church without an appointment and the secretary brought her into his office.

During this visit the woman became even more specific about all the things she wanted to do with the pastor. He explained to her that these were very wrong desires and that she needed to find a man that could be a good husband and meet her needs. But then she used the weapon that confuses most men — she began to weep. In an effort to comfort her, he went to her side and placed his hand on her shoulder. With that she rose and embraced him. From that point on things went from bad to worse. The outcome was that the woman became pregnant and was now demanding that he divorce his wife and marry her.

It was obvious to me that this pastor was sincerely repentant and would do *anything* to get his life back in order. But the big question was, *what* could he do? The woman insisted that if he didn't marry her she would announce to the congregation that he was the father of her unborn child.

I wanted to know what had led the pastor into the situation he now faced. After a life-time of trying to be a model husband, father and servant of God, what had caused this tragic error? Was he an evil man? Everything about him indicated that he was basically a man of integrity. Twelve years earlier he had come to this church when the congregation consisted of less than fifty people. He had inspired them to increase the membership to over two thousand, and had led them through two successful building programs. He and his family lived in a beautiful home and had new cars every three years. The children attended a Christian school. All this was provided by the congregation. Now he was about to lose it all — perhaps even his family and his reputation.

What had his spiritual life been like? As I questioned him, I found him sincere and consistent in his devotion to God. His weekly sermons had been used of God to win people to Christ. He was dedicated to teaching his people and he led them to seek the fruits of the Holy Spirit. What was wrong?

Since the present problem had developed because of an immoral relationship, I asked if he had ever before been unfaithful to his wife. He assured me that this was the first time since he entered the ministry that he had done anything of which he was ashamed. I picked up on his use of the word "done", so I asked him why he had used it. "Because, prior to now, I have never done anything other than think normal thoughts about other women." There it was. All he had been doing was "thinking" about other women. After about thirty years of "only thinking", his thoughts had blossomed into an act. Was the culminating action the result of the beautiful woman coming into his office? Hardly! His action came as a result of years of *thinking*. How do I know this? Because this is exactly what the Bible says in Matthew 15:19 "Out of the heart proceed evil THOUGHTS...adulteries, fornications... 20 These are the things which defile a man." The above account is not unusual. In fact, though the details might be different, similar heartbreaking scenes unfold on a regular basis throughout the Christian community.

I asked the pastor to explain what he thought the Bible

11

says about lustful thoughts. His answer indicated that he was thoroughly aware of the Biblical warnings against adultery, but that he wasn't familiar with any emphasis on our thoughts. I was surprised to learn how little this minister knew about God's requirements for pure and holy thinking. Perhaps I shouldn't say I was surprised, for I had been learning how little the average Christian knows about the importance of what we have on our minds. Do Christians *want* to know what God actually requires? It is simpler to accept the fact that we aren't perfect and to get on with going to church and doing the things that we know how to do.

Since the pastor had asked my advice, I suggested that he resign, move to a distant place and rebuild his life. He said he had reached this same conclusion, but was reluctant to leave the security of his church. The ministry was his entire life, and being a pastor was the only thing he knew. He agreed that for all concerned this was the best solution.

Months later I learned that this man had confessed his failure to his wife and that she had forgiven him. He confessed to his church, knowing the members could receive it better from him than anyone else. Did they forgive him? Probably some did and some didn't. It is very difficult for average laymen to see their pastor pushed off his pedestal. He is *supposed* to be *perfect*. Everyone knows he isn't, but at least he is supposed to give that impression.

This man now has a new occupation and is doing his best to provide for his family and for the other woman and child. He still grieves when he thinks about what he did and of the people he hurt.

I've asked the Spirit to reveal whether seeds of immorality may lie within me, waiting for an opportunity to blossom. If they are there, they will come forth! I ask you to examine your own heart under the microscope of God's Word. Do you have secret desires, hidden longings or concealed passions that are not morally pure? If so, you probably never intend for them to be activated. But any thought connected with illicit sex is like a monster waiting to take over. It can be kept hidden for many years, but at the right moment it emerges. In fact this evil force is often willing to wait for the right moment to manifest itself. It wants to damage the greatest number of people possible. Does this frighten you?

Let me assure you that I'm not talking about evil spirits *possessing* Christians. But there exists in this world an evil force whose desire is to destroy everything God wants to build. That force, Satan, is far more clever than the average Christian believes. Satan leads *his* people to live in open rebellion against God, but he is content to work secretly in the inward parts of Christians. His strategy is to entice us to want things that God has forbidden. Once the desire is created, Satan keeps fortifying that desire. He repeatedly brings it to our attention until it outweighs our desire to be obedient to God.

The pastor wanted to be obedient to God, but he had also been indulging in a dream-world — the world of his imagination. He had frequently fantasized about sex with other women. He enjoyed this world of the imagination, but never expected to *do* anything about it. I doubt if he would ever have gone out looking for a woman with whom to commit adultery. As in every case, Satan had to arrange a situation that would fit this man's personality. And Satan knows each one of us better than we know ourselves! He has had many thousands of years to observe mankind.

Most of us know people who have committed immoral acts. We have no reason to judge them, for God has strictly warned us against setting ourselves up as judges. What we *can* do is learn from their experiences. By diligently studying the Bible regarding *thoughts* and *imaginations*, we give the Holy Spirit the opportunity He seeks to cleanse our hearts.

At the close of a speaking engagement, a woman came up to me and asked for the opportunity to obtain my advice. I suggested that we sit on the front row while she shared with me. But she said her situation was so personal that we needed a more private place. An usher brought the pastor, who said we could use his office. There the woman poured out the details of the situation that was pushing her toward suicide.

This attractive and cultured lady had been a part of that church her entire life. Her father had helped to build the original church some fifty years earlier. And most of her friends and relatives were in the congregation. She was part of nearly everything that went on in the church and loved it.

The homelife she described was close to ideal. Her husband provided a beautiful home, a new car and any clothes she wanted. Their children were healthy and attending good schools. She had the freedom to come and go as she liked and was probably envied by most women who knew her.

But — and in nearly all of our lives there is a "but" — her husband was not a very warm person. He seldom showed her any affection. When she saw a man acting lovingly toward his wife, she was filled with longing. She repeatedly told herself that she would gladly exchange everything she had if she were only married to a man who would meet her physical and emotional needs. When she saw a man who looked and acted as if he were the kind of man who could make her happy, she day-dreamed about what it would be like to be married to him. The idea of experiencing passion with such a man excited and stimulated her imagination. She knew that she would *never* do anything to disrupt her home, but she continued in her fantasy. She studied different men and wondered what it would be like to have them hold her. What could be wrong with that? After all, her *actions* were always above reproach.

One evening she and her husband went to dinner at the home of their friends. During the evening the host was especially attentive to his wife. The wife seemed disinterested in her husband. The woman told me, "I couldn't help but think what a waste it was to have such a loving husband lavishing attention on a woman who didn't even care."

From that evening on she began centering her dream-world on that husband. After months of *only thinking*, she had an occasion to speak with him privately. She told him how much she admired his loving attention to his wife. He responded by telling her how much he longed for a woman who wanted him. Their discussion led to the conclusion that the two of them should have been married. This led to a warm embrace and eventually into many secret meetings.

For months they lived in agony. They couldn't stand the torment of having the person they loved living with someone else. They hated the thought of divorce, with all its ugly complications, but the man was pressing her to make a break with her husband. She understood her husband well enough to know he would *never* let her have the children. If he discovered what had been going on, he would use every resource to make sure he obtained permanent custody. She felt that losing her children might soon destroy the love she had for the other man.

The problem seemed to have only one solution. She would end her life in some way that appeared to be accidental and the whole mess would be over.

Did God look down from heaven and say to this woman, "You are living in an adulterous dream-world, therefore I am going to punish you for your disobedience"? No, I believe God longed that she recognize her world of imagination as leading into something she could not control. I believe the Holy Spirit tried to get her attention many times, but she persisted in doing what *she wanted to do.*

I wish there was a happy conclusion to this story, but there wasn't. I did the best I could, but I wasn't successful. Several months later I learned from the pastor that she had been involved in a fatal "accident" in her car.

God's laws are not designed to destroy our fun. They are designed to *protect* us. Only He knows the forces that are working against us. There is a real spirit world that has arrayed itself against God. God has made it very clear in His Word that these evil forces are powerful and that they can manipulate many things here on this earth. He repeatedly urges us to become more like His Son if we want to be protected from the painful things that evil can work in us.

The line of people across the front of the church was made up of people who were obviously in need of special prayer. Some were on crutches. One young lady was in a wheelchair. A number of people had walked to the altar in obvious pain.

When I had finished speaking, I invited those who needed prayer to come to the front. About fifty people came. Among them was a young man who stood out as someone you wouldn't expect to see in a prayer line. He was well over six feet tall, broad-shouldered, strikingly-handsome and a picture of health. I wondered what physical problem he might have.

As I prayed for the people, one by one, I noticed that the young man kept to the rear of those who had come forward. He stayed back until everyone had been prayed for and then asked if he could speak to me privately. I guided him to a quiet part of the sanctuary and, as we sat down, I asked, "What is your problem?"

The young man's composure fell apart as he tried to tell me. He had wanted to be a doctor all his life. In high school he had taken every course that would help him reach his goal. He was now in pre-medical school and was near the top of his class. Everything looked as if he were going to see his dream fulfilled.

But a few weeks earlier he had noticed symptoms in his body that worried him. Medical examinations and tests confirmed his fears — he had an incurable type of venereal disease! He hadn't been able to find out for sure whether he would be permitted to enter medical school, but the doctors who examined him doubted that he would. At this point his problem was that he couldn't concentrate on his studies. He knew his grades were sliding and his emotions

16

were running wild.

As he poured out his heart, I saw a picture of an ideal young man. He had attended church all his life and received Christ as his Saviour before he went to high school. He had never been involved with smoking, alcohol or drugs, was active in sports and had never been in any kind of trouble. But now...

He had only one affair with a young lady in his life. They attended the same church, and he had believed that he loved her. She either hadn't known she had a venereal disease or had failed to tell him. He was trying to forgive her, but he was obviously quite bitter.

We prayed, and I did my best to help him release the burden of his sickness to the Lord. His faith seemed quite weak, so I did my best to believe for him. Before we parted, I asked him what caused his present situation. His answer made it clear that he felt the cause was his failure to observe God's laws. He said he never should have had sexual relations with the young lady.

I didn't want to add to this young man's suffering, but I asked him to tell me what his thought-life had been prior to his experience with this girl. He admitted that for many years he had *wanted* to have sex with many attractive girls, but had refrained since he believed it wouldn't be right. But from his point of view, the desires he had lived with were only "natural".

It wasn't part of God's plan for this young man to have his dreams shattered. But if *anyone* follows the natural order of "the flesh", trouble will usually result. It may not be as obvious as in this case, but Satan is always careful to make the situation fit his purposes. He wouldn't want *everyone* to contract an incurable venereal disease, for then nearly everyone would be more careful. He prefers to leave it as it is, so people will always be able to believe, "It would never happen to me!"

It is *never* safe to step into Satan's territory. He goes about seeking whom he may devour. He selects his own time to accomplish his own purposes. We never know what he will do. I've had men tell me that they lived with im-

17

moral thoughts and desires for twenty-five years before they yielded to immoral acts. Time is irrelevant to Satan. If you believe that he is a reality, and that he has spiritual power, it will profit you greatly to stay out of his territory! He, too, has a plan for you and it very likely will be fulfilled if you allow any part of your life to be under his control. He is especially interested in what's on your *mind*. Ephesians 6:12 says, "We wrestle not against flesh and blood, but against principalities, against powers, against the rulers of the darkness of this world, against spiritual wickedness in high places."

During my twenty years in the Army, I was always blessed with excellent Commanding Officers. I would classify each one of them as a "good man". They tried to do their best and had a sincere interest in helping those who served under their leadership.

I became close friends with a number of my CO's, but there was one that I remember as being a dear friend. He was a Christian, active in all our chapel activities, friendly with everyone and especially intelligent. He was unusually ambitious, and one of his goals was to become a Four-Star General. He had every potential for reaching this goal. I suppose that nearly every Regular Army officer wants to become a high-ranking General Officer, but this man had an above-average zeal to succeed.

When I was in my commander's office, we would occasionally be interrupted by his secretary. She was, to say the least, a beautiful young lady. After she would leave, my boss would say things like, "Don't look at her too long, Chappie. She will get under your skin!" Or, "I have to keep my eyes off her or I will lose my convictions." It was clear that he had a *strong* attraction for this lady, but it was also clear that he had no intention of doing anything wrong.

At our staff meetings, other officers would jokingly say

such things as, "Colonel, how do you keep your hands off *that secretary* of yours?"

He would laugh, but come back with, "That lady is married and so am I. I wouldn't even come close to touching her."

On one occasion he told me he had known several officers who lost their careers because of illicit relationships with women. He said that he didn't intend to become one of the casualties. I *know* he meant it.

But — and that one word can be the prelude to a multitude of tragedies — my friend, the Commander, looked at this beautiful secretary once too often. His pent-up, inner desire eventually got the best of him, and he reached out to enjoy her. He was handsome, strong and successful, and the young lady was apparently attracted to him as well. He was never able to tell me exactly what happened, but he held his face in his hands as he asked me to pray for him so he would know how to handle the "mess" he had gotten into.

My friend resigned from the service. His dream of becoming a General Officer was destroyed. The young lady's life was severely damaged. The Army lost a superior leader. As his spiritual leader, I felt that I had failed.

That experience caused me to begin digging deeper into Scripture. I became angry with the forces that destroy good men and women, and I wanted to find ways to combat those forces. There had to be a way to defeat this "Fifth Column" activity in the hearts and lives of God's people. I was determined to find some means to help them overcome the temptation to commit adultery. My search took many years.

I spent much of my time as a chaplain and pastor trying to help myself and others fight the temptations that Satan thrusts at us. He has learned what works best, so he keeps using the same tactics. I thought that it would help if I kept reminding my congregations of the dangers we faced. I encouraged men to: go to the right places, read the right things, associate with the right people, pray much, etc. But I wasn't getting to the heart of the problem!

19

My friend, the Colonel, had a desire in his heart for that beautiful secretary. All Satan needed was time to bring that desire to the surface. I ache now as I realize how I might have helped my friend, if only I had known then what I know now. I hurt deeply when I think of the thousands of young men I might have kept from getting into hopeless situations. As a spiritual leader, I failed to present the whole truth — the entire will of God — because I didn't know what it was.

I know *now* that we must have morally clean desires. We must give up the inner, unholy longings that can be used to destroy us. And with God's help I want to use whatever abilities I have to teach men and women what we *can do*.

I pray that you will share with others the insights in this book. I especially urge you to share them with your children. Instead of worrying about the immoral influences they will have to face, patiently and prayerfully teach them what the Bible says on *thoughts* and *imaginations*. Train them to have the right kind of *desires*. It can be done!

Do everything you can to train the children in your Sunday School and church to seek pure thoughts. The traditional method of telling young people what to avoid has great merit, but it will not give them the strength they need to face the world in which they live.

After we have received Christ as our Saviour, what should happen next? During a long period in my life I was taught, and believed, that we could receive an instantaneous, transforming experience that would free us from all sin. That sounded glorious to me, but I painfully observed that many who taught and believed in this experience were as prone to commit sins as were other Christians.

I now see in the Bible God's call for every Christian to move forward into becoming more like Jesus — a call for us to strive to become holy, even as He is holy. I realize that some people cringe at the very word "holy" as if it were a term too sacred to use when referring to humans. But God has urged us to be holy, so we should squarely face that word and permit it to work in us.

God does not present this potential growth as something extremely difficult. God doesn't — but *Satan does*! He convinces Christians that holiness of any kind is so far above their reach that they might as well not even think about it. His tactics are clever, and he plays on our natural weaknesses. After all, how could we ever hope to make even a dent when there is so much that needs improving in all of us?

Once we accept this philosophy from Satan, we are content to relax and drift with the flow. If you have been "drifting", you should note that the Bible clearly states God's will for every Christian. He wants us to "strive" to enter into His will. Jesus taught us in Luke 13:24 "Strive to enter in at the strait gate: for many, I say unto you, will seek to enter in, and shall not be able."

To strive, in the Biblical sense, is not painful once we have made up our minds. It is the making up of our minds that can be *horribly* painful. It's somewhat like learning to run in a race. Who wants to go to all the work required to compete in a foot-race? But once we decide to train, and really work at winning, running can become a real joy. The non-runner might think, " Ugh. Who would want to put all that energy into running?"

If striving to become more like Jesus seems like a real drag, I promise you that it's *far* from that! It's the most thrilling thing you can *ever* do!

Jesus came to the world to help us become what God wants us to be. We have the privilege, the honor, the joy of letting His Spirit help us!

Jesus has no interest in condemning us! He only wants to bring us into fellowship with God. If you have felt condemned or worthless, it certainly wasn't He who gave you these feelings. Jesus is like a gigantic cheering section, urging us on to win. He said, "I am come that ye might have life and that ye might have it more abundantly." That is what Christian perfection is all about. It isn't giving up fun things so we can sit around and look holy. It's entering into the *excitement* of communication with God! It's learning

21

what God had in mind for the human race when He created us.

Please don't think of this book as an effort on my part to point out all the things that are wrong with you. You probably already know what's wrong. What I want to do is share how you can be delivered from wrong thoughts, so you can enter into the abundant life Jesus talked about. When He was talking to God, Jesus said in John 17:13 "I say these things while I am still in the world, so that My joy may be made full and complete and perfect in them — that they may experience My delight fulfilled in them, that My enjoyment may be perfected in their own souls, that they may have My gladness within them filling their hearts." (Amplified Version)

This book and Bible commentary is far different from anything you have ever read. You could listen to one thousand sermons and read one thousand Christian volumes and never hear one word about the central theme of this book.

As you ponder what you read, you may ask yourself why you haven't heard this message before. If the subject is as important as my comments indicate, why hasn't it been clearly proclaimed from every pulpit in the world?

If you examine the history of the Jews and Christians, you will observe that we have repeatedly ignored subjects that are of great interest to God.

The Jews had been held as slaves for four hundred years. You can believe they wanted to possess the land God had promised them. When they were on their way from their captivity in Egypt to the Promised Land, they ignored God's will for forty years. He wanted them to trust Him and not to complain. They disregarded His instructions and complained at every opportunity.

What happened? Did the earth open up and swallow them? No, they marched painfully onward, year after year. God didn't force His chosen people to stop complaining, but neither did He help them reach the Promised Land.

It is estimated that from one to three million people left Egypt, enroute to the Promised Land. Of the adults who began the journey, only two, Joshua and Caleb, ever entered into the land God had promised them. How tragic! But this is a clear lesson to you and me. The crowd *can* miss God's will. Keep that clearly in mind as you read this book. If you have been marching along with the crowd, I urge you to read the Scriptures and the comments, and you will realize that God has much to say on a subject that has been ignored for at least forty years. The Spirit is saying, "Listen carefully to what God has said!"

You and I want to enter the "land of rest" that is so clearly promised in the New Testament. Even today, few seem to enter in. Why? I believe this book will answer that question for you.

CHAPTER TWO

INCREDIBLE POWER TO IMAGINE

Your mind is somewhat like a computer. Every thought that flows through it, and every image that you create, is indelibly inscribed on the cells of your brain.

Recall some of your thoughts and created images. Then imagine them on a motion-picture screen. Would you be willing, and pleased, for that film to be shown to every Sunday School class in our land? No? Why not?

God has called us to holiness in all our thoughts. This must be our goal even when we feel too human to begin. This may seem an impossible task, but anything less falls short of what He has asked. Few Christians seem to know what it is that God has told us in His Written Word about holy thoughts.

IMAGINATION! WHAT IS IT?

It is *"The act of creating mental images of what has never been actually experienced." (Webster)*

May I reveal something that you probably never realized? Not something bad, but something good! It's something about you that is *so* good that God considers it one of your most valuable assets. In fact it's so good that if you are

25

misusing it, you will probably want to make some important changes in your life. It is your power to IMAGINE.

Have you ever considered your *incredible* power to imagine? Think of a beautiful lake with the sun shimmering on the water, trees and flowers along the shore. Can you picture it? Picture a garden filled with flowers of every color of the rainbow. Can you imagine it? Think of a giant tree reaching up into the sky and of a skyscraper stretching up to the clouds. Create in your mind a beautiful woman or a handsome man. Can you do this?

You may never have painted a picture, or planted a beautiful garden or built a building, yet you have the ability to create a picture in your mind. Have you ever pondered your power to do this? Or why you can? Has it dawned on you that this ability is God's special gift to you — you who are created in His own image? He set you apart, a jewel in the midst of all His other creations.

You may never have considered yourself as being of great value, but consider this one talent alone — your ability to imagine! Let your mind wander for a few minutes and see what you can create...See how endless your power is! Your mind is awesome in its ability. This may be the first moment in your life that you realize how incredible your imagination really is.

God values our power to imagine *far more* than any of us do. He knows why He created this power in us, and how we are designed to use it. Our creative ability is a mark of *His image* in us.

Jesus demonstrated the control that God originally intended us to have. He saw the sea and a fish with a *gold* coin in its mouth. When Peter caught the fish, sure enough, there was the gold. Jesus created it. Jesus saw pots of water becoming wine, and the water became wine. He saw bread being multiplied, and it was multiplied. He said He never did anything until He first *saw* the Father doing it (John 5:19).

Throughout history, men and women who have reported miraculous answers to prayer have repeatedly said, "I saw it before it happened." What did they mean, they "saw" it? Katherine Kuhlman frequently said things such as, "I see a person with cancer of the stomach. It is now being healed." How did she "see" it?

We "see" things all the time. Think of "white" and what do you see? Think of black, red and sunsets. As you think, you "see". But only when our power to "see" gets united with God's power to create, do we see miracles. And they happen because that is what God originally intended.

Our imaginative power received a destructive blow when man sinned against his Creator. However, in the eyes of God, our imagination is *still* a holy gift. He knows its power, even if we don't. The Bible contains many references to God's attitude toward our imagination. I've learned that He wants to help us be free of every thought that brings distress or anxiety! This potential is easily within the grasp of *everyone* reading this book. It isn't a mystical exercise that would take years to accomplish. It's a simple gift of the Holy Spirit to *any* Christian who will receive it. You do not have to be a spiritual giant or an accomplished Bible student. All you need is a sincere desire to please God.

If you carefully examine each Scripture and comment that I've included here, you will find that every part of your life — spiritual, emotional and physical — will be strengthened. No matter how strong or how weak you now are, you have in your hands a tool that will enable you to make gigantic strides forward.

I cannot over-emphasize the need to keep our imaginations under the leadership of the Holy Spirit. There is an anti-Christian movement here in the United States that centers its emphasis on the imagination. Its students are trained in the art of manipulating the imagination to the point of controlling every emotion. The trainee decides what person he wants to be and then uses images to create that person. The organization especially stresses the need to be free of moral laws, religious training and social restraints. Their code says: "Forget God, people, family,

27

friends. Be yourself. Get what you want. Learn to isolate yourself from every outside influence."

Their devotees become totally committed to selfish living. And their training isolates them from any arguments or rebuttal from friends or family.

When I realized that imagination was extremely important in God's eyes, I began to search the Scriptures to see if this could be confirmed in the Written Word. I found far more recorded information than I expected. The following are a few of the many references.

1. Genesis 6:5 "God saw that the wickedness of man was great in the earth and that every IMAGINATION of the THOUGHTS of his heart was only evil continually." The result? God destroyed the world with a flood. Man's *corrupted imagination* caused the face of the entire earth to be changed!

2. When the flood ended and Noah was able to re-establish his family on dry ground, he built an altar and made a sacrifice. God was pleased, but then it was almost as if He sighed as He looked at mankind and said in Genesis 8:21 "The IMAGINATION of man's heart is evil from his youth."

3. The next tragedy to strike the human race was the confusion of the spoken language.

Men were building the Tower of Babel, and God spoke in Genesis 11:6 "Now nothing will be restrained from them which they have IMAGINED to do."

Then in Genesis 11:7 God said "Let us go down, and there confound their language, that they may not understand one another's speech."

The pool of world knowledge was suddenly divided. After thousands of years, it is still very difficult for people of one language to communicate their thoughts and feelings to another.

When God took such drastic action, He was saying that man's imagination had the capacity to accomplish things he was *no longer* permitted to do.

In the beginning, man's boundaries were unlimited. Whatever he could imagine, he could do. Later God found it necessary to say in Genesis 31:21 "Many evils and troubles are befallen them...for I know their IMAGINATION."

Although our ability and power to imagine is a sacred gift, we have long misused it.

4. As history unfolded, God's attitude toward man's misuse of his imagination hardened, until finally in Proverbs 6:16 He said: "These six things doth the Lord hate: yea, seven are an abomination unto him."

Among this list of only seven things is: 6:18 "An heart that deviseth wicked IMAGINATIONS."

5. Frequently God spoke through the prophets to express His hatred of the misuse of imagination. In Jeremiah 23:17 "They say unto every one that walketh after the IMAGINATION of his own heart; No evil shall come upon you."

The gentle voice of our conscience may say, "You ought not to use your imagination to picture things that God has forbidden." But the evil force that corrupts says, "But you enjoy this! What harm can it do? Surely God doesn't care what you imagine. He wouldn't be *that* severe."

In Jeremiah 23:24 God asked a question: "Can any hide himself in secret places that I shall not see him? saith the Lord. Do not I fill heaven and earth?"

The carnal mind always suggests, "God isn't paying any attention to what you are thinking, and even if He does, He understands that you are merely a weak human being. After all, He made you like you are, didn't He?" This delusion entices us to forget that God made mankind in His own image. God invested Himself in man through His Son, Jesus, and proclaimed that the weakest Christian is greater than all the angels. God *"not interested"* in what we think or imagine? That is the most ridiculous thought Satan could give, yet Christians regularly accept it and imagine immoral thoughts.

Being human, we naturally ask, "Why does God *hate* an evil imagination? How do our secret thoughts hurt anyone?"

Our ability to imagine is connected with our original creation, for God said, "Let us make man in our IMAGE."

God used *His power* to create an image, and we were the result. From that point on, our power to imagine was of vital concern to God. We had part of His power invested in us.

Most scientific advancements have involved man's imagination. Men "see" things before they do them. Inventors repeatedly tell of "seeing" a machine in their imagination long before they know how to build it. Inventors awaken in the middle of the night and write out solutions to problems they have "seen" in a dream. Men see solutions in the form of pictures, and then work for years to materialize their visions. Men picture buildings in their minds and then set about making them a reality. There is something intriguing and mystifying about our ability to imagine things known and unknown. To God, that ability is sacred. He does not want it misused. And that is exactly why evil forces have an *intense* desire to see that ability misused. Our minds are the battleground; our imaginations are the trophy to be won.

If we use our imaginative power to visualize anything that represents lust or impurity, we are in *direct conflict* with God's will. Men enjoy using the power of imagination to create a multitude of images that God has forbidden. For example, when a man sees a woman who is attractive to him, he can disrobe her in his mind, bit by bit, until she is completely undressed. He then can use his imagination to feel what it would be like to touch her body. He can continue this mental activity until he has experienced every possible sexual act. He has taken God's special, holy gift and consumed it upon the altar of lust.

How do I know men do these things? First, I should confess that I engaged in such desecration of God's gift for much of my life. I continued doing this even after I became a Christian.

I have counseled with men by the hundreds on this subject, and invariably they confessed to having done the same thing most of their lives.

Married or single women are also capable of wrong thoughts, but they are usually tempted to use their imaginations in a different way. They see or think of a certain man and begin to picture life with him as their husband. They imagine his filling all their emotional and physical needs. "*He* would listen to me, *he* would talk to me, *he* would understand me." The man is coveted and mentally possessed, whether or not he is married to another woman. For a few moments he belongs to her, and once again God's precious gift of imagination has been used in direct violation of His will.

Jesus taught us that there are sins so attractive and habit-forming that even if a man came back from the dead and warned us, we would not give them up!

No sin fits this category more clearly than that of immoral thinking.

Jesus explained, in a new way, a message God presented throughout the Old Testament. He said in Matthew 5:28 "Whosoever looketh on a woman to lust after her hath committed adultery with her already in his heart."

These are not the words of a wild-eyed radical. They need to be seriously considered by every Christian, yet I believe they have been glossed over. Men and women have thought that it would be impossible to eliminate lust in their hearts, therefore Jesus must have been saying that *everyone* has lust, so no one should find fault with anyone else. I accepted this theory for most of my life, for it seemed an excellent way to handle my own moral dilemma. But now I know that Jesus is calling us to eradicate adultery from our hearts. This is what He says, and this is exactly what He means. The entire Bible is calling us to purity of heart and mind.

31

CHAPTER THREE
WHERE THOUGHTS ORIGINATE

Satan did not try to *force* Eve into disobeying God. He simply maneuvered her into *thinking* about it. He suggested the benefits she should consider.

Eve thought about them and then looked at the forbidden fruit with new interest. It looked good — but it had always looked good. The fruit hadn't changed. Only Eve's *thoughts* had changed. Satan's strategy worked then... and it is still working now!

Evil forces have skillfully and carefully conditioned the human race to believe that we are not responsible for our thoughts. Educators, "wise men" and teachers have indirectly taught that man is responsible only for what he does with thoughts that "come to him". Few have tried to explain where these thoughts originate.

I know exactly why men have tenaciously clung to the idea that it's not our fault if adulterous thoughts come into our minds. It's because of the intense physical pleasure that flash-thoughts can give. If a man can have that one flash, that one lustful moment, he is then willing to accept the teaching of Jesus and to cut off his immoral thoughts. Men have supported one another in this theology so they can continue to enjoy this brief disobedience to God.

The teaching comes in many different packages. "You can't help what you think." "After the thought comes to you, then reject it." "God will only hold you accountable if you dwell on wrong thoughts." "He knows we can't keep from having such thoughts, but He requires that we cut them off as soon as we can." All of these efforts are attempts to excuse us for directly and willfully disobeying God. Thoughts of adultery come from no place other than a man's heart. We cannot blame the opposite sex, pictures, movies or our circumstances.

If I indulge in the sin of immoral thinking, should I expect God to give me a sign, to show me I am displeasing Him? The answer to this question is found in Luke, Chapter 16, where Jesus tells the story of the rich man and of Lazarus. The rich man died and was in torment. He saw Lazarus and Abraham in the luxury of heaven, and begged Abraham for help. But Abraham had to tell him that the gulf between them was too great to cross.

The rich man pled with Abraham to get word to his five brothers, who were still alive, so they wouldn't come to the same place. Abraham's answer is in Luke 16:31 "If they hear not Moses and the prophets, neither will they be persuaded, though one rose from the dead."

The point is this: the prophets of the Old Testament and the New Testament have spoken. They have told us of God's desire that our hearts, minds and imaginations be morally pure. We can expect no further messages or miracles to persuade us. God has spoken. We have heard.

If an immoral thought is free to work in our minds for one brief second, is that wrong? In our passion for self-justification, we might declare that fallen man could not keep such one-second thoughts out of his mind. But consider that one second from *God's* perspective. How long is a second to Him? The Bible says one period of time can be as one thousand to Him! At that ratio an immoral thought that seems to be one second to us could be over an hour to God!

But, of course, time is not the issue at all. God requires clean, pure, holy thoughts, and our objective must be to become what *He wants*, regardless of how violently our

34

fallen natures may resist. And be sure they *will* resist! If you have spent many years enjoying flash, one-second immoral thoughts, you will not easily give up this pleasure.

I've often heard expressions like, "If a bird lands on your head, you don't have to let it make a nest there." The point being that when a thought comes we don't have to retain it and mull over it. This is true. It is wrong to have an evil thought and then to keep meditating on it. The more we think about it, the worse it becomes, and the greater our guilt becomes.

But why have the thought in the first place?

At this point, I can hear the cries of those who will say, "No one can control the thoughts that flash into his mind. He can only refuse to meditate on them."

Since little has been written on the subject of continuing in lustful thoughts after they come to us, perhaps I would be wise to simply write about that aspect of our thought-life. But if I did this, I would not be faithful to what I believe the Holy Spirit is telling me, nor would I be honestly reporting what the Bible says.

The following are a few of the Scriptures which make it clear that Christians are responsible for thoughts that come to their minds for *any* length of time.

1. Psalm 139:23 "Search me, O God and know my heart: try me, and know my THOUGHTS: 24 And see if there be any wicked way in me." The implication is that David had reached a new spiritual plateau in his walk with God. Once, his thoughts had led him into adultery and then to murder. Now he is inviting God to let him know if *any* of his thoughts are wicked.

2. I Corinthians 13:11 "When I was a child I spoke as a child, I understood as a child, I thought as a child: but when I became a man; I put away childish things."

Paul is talking about spiritual progress. That is what this book is about. Let us renounce the idea that Christians cannot control what they think. If we accept that approach, we will never be victorious in Christ. Such a philosophy insists that, if a thought comes to you for one second, you aren't responsible. But what happens eventually?

35

You know what happens! It stays for two seconds, then three. Year after year the pattern is reinforced. It's time for us to learn how to cut off evil *before* it begins, and then reap the rich rewards of minds cleansed by the power of His Word.

3. Matthew 9:4 "And Jesus knowing their THOUGHTS said, Wherefore THINK ye evil in your hearts?"

The scribes hear Jesus forgiving people of their sins, and the thought comes to their minds, This is blasphemy. They don't accuse Him. They simply "think". Jesus then asks them why they are *thinking* evil. He clearly is holding them responsible for their thoughts. I strongly recommend that you accept the fact that Jesus will one day hold you and me accountable for *our* thoughts — every one of them.

4. Romans 8:6 "For to be carnally MINDED is death; but to be spiritually MINDED is life and peace." It would be foolish for us to think, I have carnal thoughts but I am not "carnal". Peace of mind comes only to those who learn to have "spiritual" thoughts.

5. Philippians 2:5 "Let this MIND be in you, which was also in Christ Jesus."

Do you believe Jesus' mind was *perfectly* pure? He was "equal with God"! We are called by God to have the mind of Christ. Later in this chapter, Paul exhorts in verse 12, "Work out your own salvation with fear and trembling." Verse 15, "That ye may be blameless and harmless, the sons of God, without rebuke, in the midst of a crooked and perverse generation." Moral decay is sweeping over our nation to a degree that is almost unbelievable. Lust and immorality are portrayed as acceptable. If Christians do not cling to purity of thought we will be swept into the morass of corruption.

We have a source of assistance, as emphasized in Joshua 1:8 "This book of the law shall not depart out of thy mouth; but thou shalt meditate therein day and night, that thou mayest observe to do according to all that is written therein: for then thou shalt make thy way prosperous, and then thou shalt have good success." (Want to be prosper-

36

ous and have good success?) And also Psalm 119:9 "Wherewithal shall a young man cleanse his way? by taking heed thereto according to thy word. 11 Thy word have I hid in mine heart, that I might not sin against thee."

6. Titus 1:15 "Unto the pure all things are pure: but unto them that are defiled and unbelieving is nothing pure; but even their MIND and conscience is defiled." Paul is not saying that if the pure in heart see a murder, they will think it is pure. He *is* saying that if we are defiled in our minds we can look at anything and make it impure. If our thoughts are defiled, our mind and conscience become defiled. We can then repeat the same evil thoughts, time after time, without any strong sense of guilt.

7. Deuteronomy 18:6 "If a Levite come...with all the desire of his MIND...then he shall minister in the name of the Lord." Have you known that God wants *all* the "desires of your mind" if you want to serve Him?

8. Ezekiel 11:5 "I know the things that come into your MIND, every one of them. 12...ye have not walked in my statutes, neither executed my judgments, but have done after the manners of the heathen that are round about you." There is no more glaring illustration of God's people following after the ways of the heathen than if we think adulterous thoughts.

Let's move on to another illustration. My doctor placed me on a strict diet that allowed me to eat nothing but meat and vegetables. Meditate on this for a moment, and you will realize how *many* foods are not meat or vegetables.

My mind was craving a certain food that was not on my diet. I would wake up thinking about it. A dozen times a day the thought would come, "I sure would enjoy some of that to eat." The food itself was not bad. The desire to eat wasn't bad. The problem was that I was being tormented by the *thought*. The Holy Spirit spoke to me: "Merlin, you have listened to me and allowed me to help you defeat the power of immoral thinking. Now I will teach you something new. You do not have to think about wanting that food."

37

My reaction was, "I must be hearing my own desires." (I have learned that this can happen to any one of us very easily!)

The voice insisted that I *was* receiving an important lesson and that I should listen.

My answer was, "But I can't help it!"

"GOD HAS GIVEN YOU AUTHORITY OVER YOUR THOUGHTS.
YOU CAN DECIDE WHAT YOU WANT TO THINK."

This was quite a revelation to me — perhaps one of the biggest in my entire life.

A little later, I realized the same thought was coming back to me — the desire for *that food*. I tried what the Spirit had told me, and to my absolute amazement it worked! I could think of the food and then literally cut off the thought of wanting it! This was an exciting moment, for I knew I was experiencing something that to me was completely new.

I confess that my faith wasn't too strong at that point. I wondered how long I could use this ability to control what I was thinking about the food. But as the same experience came to me many times that day, and each time I was successful in cutting off my *desire* for it, I realized what a blessing the Holy Spirit had given me. I'm not saying that being able to shut off the desire for a food is such a big thing. The point is that God wants to restore in us the power to *control the thoughts that flow through our minds*. I believe that when He created mankind, men and women had total control over what they thought. Through the "fall", we lost that ability, and now the Holy Spirit wants to help us "renew our minds". It is exciting to realize the potential God has given us in many areas of our lives!

I do not mean that I now have instant control over *every* thought. It's a matter of learning and growing. I now seem to be learning something new every day. Yesterday, a carpenter examined a shower in our home and told me it had been leaking through the drain and under the floor —

probably for many years. As he took up the linoleum, he discovered that the floor, and possibly the material under the floor, had rotted away. He recommended that the entire shower be taken out, replaced and a new floor put in. When he told me the estimated cost, my first thought was, "Oh, what a waste." I really wasn't too happy about it. Eventually I would have realized that God would make it work for my good, but for a few minutes I was burdened by the whole thing.

But then the Holy Spirit witnessed to me, "You don't have to accept that unhappy thought." And the moment I rejected the thought it was gone!

There was a time, as a Christian, that I had many lustful thoughts. I honestly thought I could not help myself. I knew that I did not want to actually commit adultery, but I *did want* to imagine and think about it. As the Holy Spirit dealt with me, He urged me to pray that the thoughts of my mind might be cleansed. It wasn't easy! I was indulging in a practice that had started in my mind when I was a young boy. These thoughts became part of me. They seemed to control me, rather than my controlling them. I don't mean I thought lustful thoughts all the time, but in certain situations these thoughts would explode into my conscious mind.

During the years that immoral thoughts flowed through my mind, I always felt guilty, but I was never overly-worried. I guess what kept me from being too concerned were conversations I had with other Christian men. I came to the conclusion, and still believe, that a vast majority have the same difficulty.

What is written here may cause some wails of agony within the Christian community, but many Christians will rejoice that these hidden matters are being brought to light. Those who have felt a burden in their hearts for many years, will *now* realize that their secret thoughts are being condemned by God. As the Holy Spirit helps them to renew their minds, they will experience new victory in Christ. Christians will be set free and then with new enthusiasm go on to win others to Christ.

Often, men and women have an inner sense of unworthiness. They may think it's because they lack education, or special talents, or because of some weakness beyond their control. Frequently, the problem lies in their immoral thought-life. This saps and drains away spiritual life, until they are powerless to help themselves and others. But by cleansing our thoughts, we open the door to many things the Holy Spirit wants to do in our lives.

Keep your mind open to the Scriptures in this book. If you have been guilty of thoughts such as, "I wish that man were my husband", think carefully about the Scripture, "Thou shalt not covet." The commandment means we are not to *want* someone else's husband or wife. God would never have outlawed covetousness if He didn't know He had given us control over our thoughts.

If a husband is mentally committing adultery with Raquel Welch, how can his wife ever come up to his expectations?

If a wife visualizes herself as Raquel Welch and is hostile to the plain Joe Blow she is married to, what chance does the marriage have? This wife needs to look in the mirror and ask, "What does he see when he comes home? You are not Raquel and Robert Redford isn't coming home."

If a wife saturates herself in daily soap-operas that are loaded with glamorized illicit sex, she is creating in her mind a desire for immorality. Soon that mental desire will become a desire of her heart. Without realizing what is happening, she will take on the desires of the characters she is watching. Why not? She is watching what she *desires* to see.

If a wife learns to fantasize her emotional life by reading many romantic novels, she may not be able to adapt to real life. Novels often depict a wife in a beautiful romantic setting. The heroine is encircled with opportunities to be glamorous, beautiful, popular, witty and desirable. The reader may spend her days washing diapers, cleaning the same house and coping with the same problems day after day. But her mind becomes steeped in an imaginary world until eventually the desire of her heart is to escape her real world. Her marriage may develop serious problems since no man can compete with men who are the product of someone's imagination.

If you become convinced that the Bible demands strict moral thoughts, will you conform?

If you have a strong desire to conform to Biblical standards, will you?

The answer to both questions is, *maybe*.

The mind is amazingly deceptive. It can find unlimited ways of excusing whatever it wants to do. It can say, "Yes, the Bible demands purity of thought, but I'm not perfect. Who is?" Or, "Yes, I have a strong desire to do everything the Bible requires of me, but in this case I can't. My mind is not controllable."

Neatly, the mind has side-stepped the issue. It has excused its actions so it can continue to do what it enjoys.

The truth is, we think what we want to think. The Bible makes us personally responsible for *every* thought we have. We are not computers, programmed to respond to forces beyond our control. We were created by God, in His image, as free moral agents. This is precisely why God says, "Every one of us shall give account of himself to God" (Romans 14:12).

The alcoholic continues to drink because he wants to. He may be aware that his body is suffering from the effects of alcohol, but he finds some way to excuse his acts.

The person misusing drugs may know his body and mind are being destroyed, but he thinks, I can't help myself.

The Christian who thinks immoral thoughts usually knows he is damaging his spirit. He feels guilty and wouldn't want anyone to know, but he thinks, I can't help myself.

Are you aware how often immoral thoughts involve the mental disrobing of the body? This takes us back to man's original sin. What was the first thought that came to Adam and Eve after they had sinned? They realized they were naked!

Rebellion against God opened a new consciousness. The unclothing of the body is still rebellion against God, if it is

41

done in ways He has forbidden. Satan has always used the human body as a way to foster rebellion, and thus to damage the human spirit. He uses countless methods to convince us that even if we wound and hurt our spirits by immoral thoughts, we are not responsible.

Man has never been clever enough to disobey God and not eventually suffer the consequences. So often men think, I've thought wrong thoughts many times, and nothing drastic happened. God is patient, kind and long-suffering, but He cannot violate His own word. "Whatsoever a man soweth that shall he also reap" (Galatians 6:7).

Have you already observed that your natural mind does not want to be controlled by God? The Bible puts it this way in Romans 8:7 "The carnal mind is enmity against God."

It's a little heavy to realize that our own mind is God's enemy. There are many illustrations of this. You may have observed some of them working in your own life:

1. God says we are to, "Rejoice in Him *always*." Our mind says, "I will rejoice when I feel like it."

2. God says that whatever we eat or drink should be done to glorify Him (I Cor 10:31). The mind says, "If I like it or want it, I'll eat it." What a tremendous change would take place in many people's eating habits if their diets were controlled by that which would give glory to God!

3. God says that if we think another person has done wrong, we should *first* go to that person and discuss their acts with them. The mind says, "Quick, find someone and tell them what you have just heard."

4. God says to honor those who have rule over us. The mind says, "I'll honor them if they are in my political party, and if I like them and if I agree with what they do."

5. God says to thank Him for *everything* (Eph 5:20). The mind says, "I'll thank Him for whatever I like, and complain about whatever I don't like."

6. God says, "Fear not." The mind causes most people to be afraid, dozens of times a day, about things that never happen. But the mind says, "Well, they *might* happen."

7. God says He will work everything for our good (Rom 8:28), and in the same chapter He lists some of the things He will use for our good: tribulation, distress, persecution, famine, nakedness, peril, sword (atomic bombs?), death, life, angels, principalities, powers, things present (which would include everything), things to come (eliminating the need to be afraid), height, depth, any other creatures (things).

The mind says, "I don't believe it."

8. God says, "Love others — even your enemies." The mind says, "I will love those I like."

9. God says, "Don't covet." The mind says, "Ridiculous. How can I keep from wanting something that I want?"

CHAPTER FOUR

OUR MOST CONSUMING TEMPTATION

In l971, I completed a cumulative twenty years of service in the military. I was ready to retire. What a sweet word that was to my ears. In every way I was ready to retire. They had been a long and rugged twenty years — perhaps far more so than the average civilian realizes. During those years, I had seen hundreds of men dying around me — on battlefields around the world. I was one of the favored-few. I survived. Others who "survived" with me were without legs, blind, deaf or armless. Some had multiple losses. But I had survived, and I was ready to retire.

I looked back over my past and realized why I felt so tired. World War II had been a traumatic experience. Many of my closest friends had died as we, the members of the famed 82nd Airborne Division, fought our way through Europe. When I was discharged from the Army in 1946, the very last thing I ever wanted to do was have any part in the military.

By 1953 the Lord convinced me that He had other plans. At His direction, I went back into the Army as a chaplain. Just for three years — I thought! Three years was extended as the Holy Spirit convinced me my work wasn't completed. Then came Korea, where I saw more death. In the Dominican Republic I had the painful assignment of helping to load into planes, dead soldiers from the 82nd Airborne Division. Their bodies were to be sent back to their

45

families. Then came a grueling, exhausting year in Vietnam. In ninety-seven-degree temperature and ninety-seven-percent humidity, I watched hundreds of soldiers pay a colossal price for our country's mistakes.

By 1971 I had completed *Prison to Praise*. Everything I knew about anything was written down, and I was ready to retire. And retire I did. But the Holy Spirit kept prodding me, and from within came *Power in Praise*. Now surely I was finished and could actually retire.

But then letters began pouring in from all over the world. People were being helped by my books, but they had many questions. The Holy Spirit urged me to answer their questions as best I could. Prisoners all over the United States were given copies of my first two books, and they were writing things like, "Are you a real person? Are your books true or just stories?" I had to answer them. They were living, hurting people. Out of all these letters came a new book, *Answers to Praise*. I was *certain* that this would end my writing career. But, like *Prison to Praise* and *Power in Praise*, *Answers to Praise* rose to the Ten Best-Selling Christian Book list. More letters poured in from many places. No time for retirement; too many people were asking for help; too many churches were inviting me to come and share the message of praise.

Then came a call to build a church in Southern California. "But Lord, I've already built dozens of churches all over the world."

"Go do it," was all I heard. As told in *Walking and Leaping*, my work in that church ended, and I expected to really retire. But over seven-hundred people left that church and urged me to begin another new church. No retirement, and two more books *had to be* written.

After this church was established and a building purchased, the Lord led me to resign. Now I was *ready to retire*. This was it. No more churches to build and maybe no more books to write.

But now another book is being born. I believe God is using my previous experiences to help us learn the importance of what is on our minds.

Many Christian men have told me that when they first accepted Christ, their minds were made clean. They could look at beautiful women and every thought was pure.

Days, weeks or perhaps months later, when an impure thought entered, they held on to it for just a second or two. The thought stirred old memories, and the old desires began to reassert themselves. For a time, these occasional immoral thoughts brought strong feelings of guilt; gradually the conscious guilt declined. These men eventually decided that even Christian men cannot be expected to be pure in heart. They were not aware that the guilt feelings were still there, working their way deeper and deeper into their hearts.

During my time in the military, I was at the side of many Christian men who believed they were dying. When I asked them what they would like me to pray for, in nearly every case they asked me to pray that they would be forgiven for past sins. When I asked what specific sins they wanted to confess to God, their first thoughts were frequently about the men they had been forced to kill in their roles as soldiers. Their next requests were usually about immoral acts or thoughts.

The point is, we can hide our guilt over impure thoughts even from ourselves, but in times of great danger, problems, stress or death, what is hidden in the heart will surface.

Women report similar experiences. After receiving Christ, their lives are more content. Jesus meets their needs. But later, old desires begin to surface. They remember, see or meet men who "really could meet their needs".

Sometimes when men and women seek a new relationship with the Holy Spirit, their expectations are even higher, and their guilt even greater, when immoral thoughts creep back into their minds.

Sooner or later, we have to face the reality that God has given *us* the responsibility of cleansing the thoughts of our hearts. The Holy Spirit and God's Word are available to help us, but each person must decide for himself what he will think, and what he will imagine. Being created in God's image *requires* that we be responsible for our thoughts.

Why do men and women think immoral thoughts?
Because they want to!
And they want to because they enjoy it.
These thoughts bring physical pleasure to the body.
The sensations are pleasant and gratifying.

The mind becomes programmed to renew this pleasure at the slightest provocation. In time, the mind needs no stimulus — it can create its own. Self-gratification becomes habitual and seemingly uncontrollable. But man is *always* responsible for his thoughts, because he is made in God's image. God has said, "As he THINKETH in his heart, so is he" (Prov 23:7).

There is a remedy! "The Word of God is quick and powerful and sharper than any two edged sword...and is able to discern the thoughts and intents of the heart" (Heb 4:12). If any man wants to continue enjoying immoral thinking, he must keep his mind *off* the Scripture verses that are recorded in this book. They are "powerful and able to pierce" the wall we build around our hearts. Once that wall is in place, we are able to think, "What I'm doing isn't really wrong."

Thousands of men have told me that their most consuming and overpowering temptation is immoral thinking. Many men declare that this problem gives them a sense of guilt that torments them dozens of times every day. They assert that the temptation toward immorality is stronger than *all other* temptations put together. Christian men frequently say that their wives have little idea how traumatic the conflict is between their desire to be morally pure and the seductive influence of adulterous thoughts. Men would be even more concerned if they realized that when the mind is permitted the freedom of immoral thinking, it will eventually find ways to excuse immoral acts!

Some women report a different type of problem — a longing that causes them to want a different man — one who would meet their emotional needs.

Is there a solution? Yes, there is!
Men *and* women must first realize the seriousness of the

48

problem. All too often immoral thinking is considered uncontrollable. A man excuses his thoughts with the rationalization that he is merely doing what every other man does. But once we understand what Scripture says on the subject, realize how important our minds are to God and permit His words to penetrate our hearts, we *can* be set free.

"In the beginning God created...And God said, Let us make man in our image...male and female created He them." We are a part of God. He invested His image in us. I had read this verse hundreds of times, and I confess that it hadn't made too much of an impression on me.

Earlier in my Christian walk I received a beautiful gift from God. He emptied my mind of *all* lustful thoughts. I expected that cleansing to be permanent — and it could have been. But I neglected one important thing. I didn't keep renewing my mind with the spiritual resources God has provided in His Word. Gradually, and without my making a conscious decision to disobey God, the old thoughts began creeping back into my mind.

One day I was disturbed because of my immoral thoughts. I had been disturbed many times, but on this particular day my heart was especially heavy. From somewhere deep within I was crying out, "Oh God, please help me. I know my bad thoughts are in disobedience to You, but I can't seem to help myself. I think things about women, and I'm deeply ashamed. I don't want to do this." I really *wanted* to give up this sin.

I didn't hear God speak to me audibly, but I sensed His asking me, "Do you *really* want to be helped? If I help you, then you will be far more accountable for what you do in the future."

I was able to make a decision, and I cried out, "Oh please, God, help me."

He said to me, "The answer is in My Word."

"I know Lord, but where?"

"Look!"

And I began to look. What better place to look than at the very beginning of His Word? There it was, "In the beginning God created." When we look at the opposite sex, we are looking at a part of God — *His creation*! When it dawned on me what the Spirit was revealing, I was so frightened I began to shake. I had been looking at God's creation and lusting for an adulterous relationship with what was a part of Him. For awhile, I found it difficult to breathe. The Word of God was piercing my heart, and it was indeed quick and powerful. Even though I had known for many years *what* the Word said, it had only now begun to reveal the thoughts of my heart.

The secret of learning how to have a clean mind requires two things:

1. Learn what the Bible says about the mind.

2. Let God's words move from our minds down into our hearts. To me the heart means the center of the person I am. That "center" has to be convinced before I will make any important changes in my life.

When I meditated on the significance of what I had learned, I gradually understood the drastic pronouncement Jesus had made: "If thine eye offend thee, pluck it out: it is better for thee to enter into the kingdom of God with one eye, than having two eyes to be cast into hell fire" (Mk 9:47). In the book of Matthew, Jesus went so far as to say that even *wanting* adultery was in fact an act of adultery in God's eyes. "Whosoever looketh on a woman to lust after her hath committed adultery with her already in his heart" (Mt 5:28).

As I've shared my new understanding of what Jesus said, many have told me it was so powerful that they were instantly shocked into making a commitment to completely abandon immoral thoughts.

When a man or woman accepts Jesus as Saviour, they are told in John 14:23 " We will come into him, and make our abode with him." If a man looks on a woman who has *God living in her*, and has adulterous thoughts, he is actually wanting to commit adultery *with God's Temple*!! Understanding this helps me see why the Bible has so much to say about adultery, immorality and evil thoughts. Satan wants man to lust after God!

If a man wants to be delivered from immoral thinking, he has abundant resources. The Bible has so much to say about God's will in this matter, that if we meditate on these Scriptures, our resolve will be greatly strengthened.

It is increasingly evident to me that Christian men do not realize the importance that God places on both morality in actions *and* purity in thoughts. My discussions with men verify that few have an adequate understanding of how much the Bible has to say about this subject. I have therefore felt impelled by the Spirit to put these scriptural references into a convenient, handy form that men can easily read. If a man has even a slight interest in being morally clean, these verses can set him free. But they must be received into the "heart" and meditated upon regularly. If a man refuses to keep his attention on the resources that God has given, he will probably be lured back into the darkness and hopelessness of immorality. If he meditates on these words frequently, I believe the Holy Spirit will provide all the strength he needs to flee this sin which God has spoken against so strongly. In John 15:3 He said "Now are ye clean through the word which I have spoken unto you."

Our minds are comparable to a radio. We pick up a message that says, for example, "I want a hot fudge sundae." Exactly what is it that "wants" and where does the thought originate? Does the body need this for health? Will it improve the body's ability to enjoy tomorrow? Probably not.

What process does the mind go through to reach the conclusion, "I want"? Previous experiences that brought pleasure? Anticipation?

If we understand the process that leads us to want something, then we may be able to control what we will want in the future.

If we say, "I want a hot fudge sundae," that is an honest expression of our desire. How can we change that desire?

If our doctor says, "You *may* have diabetes," that gives us some incentive to change what we desire to eat. One person could hear this from his doctor and immediately be in-

51

spired to completely change his diet to exclude all refined sugar. Another person wouldn't even consider changing.

If our doctor says, "You *have* diabetes and need to change your eating habits," we have quite a strong reason to change our desires and might even be to the point where we *do not* want a hot fudge sundae. But, strange as it may seem, some persons would continue eating whatever they wanted.

If our doctor says, "You have a severe case of diabetes and refined sugar could put you into shock," a person with reasonable intelligence should give careful thought to his future diet!

There is a comparable mental process in other decisions we make. A mind that says, "I want to have immoral thoughts" can be changed. What might change it?

A Scripture verse that says immoral thoughts are wrong? Maybe.

Several verses that say God does not want thoughts to be impure? A better chance of getting our attention.

Dozens of Scripture verses that clearly say immoral thoughts and desires are forbidden by God and that He may bring severe suffering on those who disobey? This should get and hold the attention of a reasonable person.

Receiving Christ as Saviour is much more than accepting Him with our minds. It must also be a decision of our hearts. The decision must be so permanent and binding on the individual that it becomes more than a mental assent that Christ is divine, or that He is The Saviour. The decision is a complete surrender of self to Jesus as Lord.

Accepting the Holy Spirit as Lord of our thinking habits is more than a mental decision. It must be a complete surrender of our hearts. This decision commits us to a permanent stand against immoral thoughts. Once this complete commitment is made, the Holy Spirit then moves to help us do whatever we cannot do for ourselves.

When you gave your life to Christ, wasn't it a complete commitment to believe in Him as Saviour — forever? Your total commitment made your conversion real. You didn't promise not to fall. God didn't ask you to do that. But you did promise to believe in Jesus as Saviour, without any reservations, for now and forever.

When we commit our minds to holy thoughts, we are submitting our minds to the Holy Spirit's control. This opens the way for a life of service to God and closes the door to the untold suffering that comes when we are disobedient to Him.

You may wonder, "What happens if I make a commitment to God to think only clean thoughts, and then slip back into my old thoughts?" The answer is found in the very encouraging promise in I John 1:9 "If we confess our sins, he is faithful and just to forgive us our sins." John also assures us that when Jesus sets us free, we are free indeed! And who wants to leave freedom to return to bondage?

CHAPTER FIVE

WHEN WILL THERE BE A SPIRITUAL REVIVAL?

Have you ever been around a person who gave you confidence, who made you feel that the situation was under control? Some people seem to be born leaders. Others follow without questioning.

If a human being has the potential to create confidence, how much greater is the Holy Spirit's capability! But the Holy Spirit is not pushy. He wants us to *accept* His leadership. Then He wants to lead us into thinking holy thoughts regardless of how far we are now from reaching that goal.

When the Roman Centurion expressed his faith in Jesus, He responded as recorded in Matthew 8:10 "I have not found so great faith, no not in Israel."

The Centurion believed that Jesus could heal, but that wasn't why Jesus praised him so highly. Many people believed He could heal. This Roman officer understood something about Jesus that *no one* else had! What was it?

This soldier compared Jesus' authority over sickness to his own authority over servants. He, the Centurion, could tell his servants to do something, and they did it. He had absolute authority over their lives. If they should dare to refuse his command, he could order them to be immediately executed. This is *real authority*!

The Centurion was saying that he knew Jesus had this same authority over sickness. Even though illness seemed to have great power, he knew Jesus was more powerful than the forces that caused sickness.

We know that evil forces are inciting immorality throughout the world. The results are devastating. It would be impossible to measure the pain and suffering being experienced as a direct result of immorality. Consider venereal diseases with all their ramifications: blindness, heart disease, birth defects that stay with a child for a *lifetime*, emotional agony, suicide and divorce. The list is endless. Consider prostitution with all its tragedies: white slavery that causes thousands of innocent young girls to disappear every year, crime associated with pimps, graft, beatings, threats and blackmail. Consider divorces that are caused by immorality: children deprived of a wholesome home, poverty, emotional collapse.

Consider the rapid increase of suicide among young people. They are presented the delusion that immorality will satisfy all their desires. They try it and discover that, rather than improving their lives, it actually results in a feeling of futility. If illicit sex, which is supposed to be the most desirable thing in life, turns out to be unfulfilling, what then is there to live for? Nothing, some say, and so there is one more suicidal sacrifice to the god of this world.

Today, how many followers of Jesus realize that He has authority over immoral thinking? Contrary to the opinions of a multitude of Christians, we do not have to live under the authority of lust and immoral desires! We *can* and *should* be free! Jesus provides that freedom. And freedom from immoral thinking is *far more important* than physical healing. Lust is a sin of the heart. Jesus said that out of the heart proceed evil thoughts (Mt 15:19). It is believed by an increasing number of authorities that most physical illness is caused by wrong diet. But the more dangerous sickness — immorality of thought — comes from the heart.

You may have observed the present emphasis on healing of the physical body. Sermons by the thousands are preached, telling people how they can be healed. Books are written by the hundreds on this subject. Many are helped by these ministries, and all of this has a part in pointing people to Christ as Saviour. But how many sermons and books deal with holy thoughts and desires? It seems that this subject has been ignored because it is considered either unimportant or impossible. Since it certainly isn't unimportant from a biblical perspective, it must then be considered impossible. Or perhaps it is considered too unpopular a subject with which to deal. Most of us are not likely to get excited over any effort to uncover our hidden thoughts!

Great emphasis is now being placed on abortions, but abortion is a by-product of immoral thinking! Man must first have something in his heart, before he puts it into action. The Bible repeatedly emphasizes that our first and foremost concern should be the spiritual condition of our hearts.

Many Christians reach a plateau in their spiritual lives and seem to be able to go no further. They pray, study the Bible, attend church regularly, tithe, memorize Bible promises, and keep trying to grow in faith. But they stay at the same level year after year. Any resemblance to your situation?

Sooner or later, all Christians must come to realize that God is not foolish! He has filled the Bible with many generous promises of all the things He will do for His children. But He was wise enough to build perfect controls into His Word. We can obtain only limited answers to our prayers until we learn to *keep His Word*! Many Christians put a lifetime of effort into trying to ''release faith'' to get God's promises, while they are refusing to *keep* His Word. Impossible! We can't use miracle-working faith if we refuse to follow God's directions. It doesn't matter how enthusiastically someone tells us that we can receive *everything* from God simply by claiming His promises. It simply isn't true — which you may have already discovered. Every promise of God is conditioned on our obedience. Jesus clearly said that *He* received everything He prayed for because *He* always did God's will. I'm thankful there are some things God will give us even when we are disobedient. But He will not give us, for example, power to work miracles until we know how to wisely use that power.

The following Scriptures emphasize this point.

1. John 15:7 "If ye abide in me, and my words abide in you, ye shall ask what ye will, and it shall be done unto you."

Being in Christ's will is clearly a requirement for receiving from God.

2. I John 3:22 "And whatsoever we ask, we receive of him because we keep his commandments and do those things that are pleasing in his sight."

Pure desires are certainly pleasing in God's sight!

3. James 4:3 "Ye ask, and receive not, because ye ask amiss, that ye may consume it upon your lusts. 4. Ye adulterers and adulteresses."

Didn't Jesus make it clear that adultery in the heart was as destructive as the act of adultery? Doesn't this verse make it clear that God will not give us blessings that will be enjoyed in the midst of our lusts?

4. James 4:8 "Purify your hearts, ye double minded."

Note that He doesn't say, "Ask Me to purify you," but rather, "*You* purify." This means we are capable, and we cannot expect miraculous answers to prayers until we *do* purify our hearts.

God makes this so clear, yet people vainly seek an easier way. They go to hear anyone who will tell them it is easy to receive health and wealth if they will only believe . It *is* easy to receive from God, but only if we come to Him while we are doing what we can to purify the desires of our hearts. Of course we will never be *perfect*, but our goal must be obedience to Him. His goals for us are clarified in:

1. Leviticus 20:7 "Sanctify yourselves therefore, and be ye holy."

2. Ephesians 1:4 "We should be holy and without blame before him."

3. II Corinthians 7:1 "Let us cleanse ourselves from all filthiness of the flesh and spirit, perfecting holiness in the fear of God."

4. Hebrews 12:4 "Follow...holiness, without which no man shall see the Lord."

You have heard the adage, "Half a glass of water is seen

as either half-full or half-empty." You can see these verses and this book as a pronouncement that you are half-empty, *or* you can see them as a great blessing. You are learning how you can be full!

If our spiritual lives are in a rut, and we are trying method after method, prayer after prayer — year after year — there is only one way that will work — seeking holiness of heart, mind, soul and imagination. God will honor every step we take toward becoming what He wants us to be.

Many books have been written and many sermons preached exhorting us not to: commit adultery, steal, hurt others, drink alcohol, etc. We have also been frequently told to: go to church, help others, care for our families, study the Bible, etc. All of these are good things, but if we never *do* wrong and always *do* good, we will still be a long way from the holiness described in the Bible.

In this generation, little has been written or taught about our need to be pure in heart, thought and imagination. The Bible is filled with God's exhortations to be pure in our desires and thoughts. It is in these areas that the real victories are won.

To concentrate our energies on what men *do*, is like sending all our fire-fighting equipment outside the city to put out brush fires, when the heart of the city itself is burning down!

The hearts of Christians are being corrupted by the world in which we live. Men and women are being sucked into the filth of lustful, adulterous, covetous thinking, and the only warning Christians are receiving, is to not *do* any of the physical acts! Of course we are not supposed to do the acts, but we shouldn't be indulging in the thoughts either.

IMMORAL THINKING DRAINS AWAY THE SPIRITUAL POWER WE SHOULD HAVE. Satan knows this, and he uses his most skillful tactics to keep our inner decay from being called exactly what it is — disobedience to God.

How do I know there is spiritual decay in Christians' hearts? Everywhere I have spoken on this subject, the audience has confirmed what I'm telling you. Immorality in the minds of Christians is rampant! Holiness of desire, as taught by Jesus and His disciples, is almost unknown.

Spiritual leaders are often caught in the same web, and are therefore unable to say anything about the dangerous condition we are in. How do I know this? I'm not just making a statement of what I *think* may be true. I'm reporting what men and women in positions of leadership have been telling me for many years!

Many men are predicting an outpouring of the Holy Spirit upon our nation in the near future. I wish that I could unite with others in these enthusiastic expectations, but I am unable to do so.

My understanding of Scripture leads me to believe that God will pour out His Spirit upon us as His Spirit controls us. My conviction is that here in the United States we are moving *further away* from obedience.

In writing this prediction, I know I am going against the mainstream of what is being said and written. The United States will not have a great revival until there are changes in the hearts of Christians. At present, there is moral decay that will prevent our country, and much of the world, from entering into the good things God has prepared for us.

But there is no need for discouragement! The Holy Spirit is ready to minister His fullness to each one of us as *we* are ready. If we are willing for Him to control the desires of our hearts, He is willing to work God's perfect will in our lives. We do not have to center our attention on what other people are doing or not doing.

As individual Christians are changed into the likeness of Christ, we will see the moving of the Holy Spirit throughout our land. This makes the future contingent on our spiritual progress rather than God's set time when he will sovereignly pour out His Spirit. When I examine the history of God's dealings with the human race, I see the Lord doing His part as man acts in obedience to His Word. The Bible promises a special work of the Holy Spirit in the latter days, but the Word also says there will be a purifying of hearts in believers.

If the Body of Christ in our country does not seek holiness of heart, there will be further decay, and the freedom of religion we now enjoy will be gone. This has happened in nation after nation since the beginning of time, and we have no reason to expect anything different. God turned His back on disobedient Israel time after time. They came under slavery for as long as four hundred years! The same thing could happen to our nation.

Do I see signs of increasing decay in the hearts of Christians? I do. Moral and spiritual filth is being accepted into homes — through television — that fifty years ago would have caused Christians to react as Jesus did when He saw the temple being desecrated. We are being conditioned to accept *anything*. God will not tolerate this indefinitely.

This book is my effort to come against the forces that are striving to pollute our thoughts and desires. Noah warned the people of his day that God was angry. If Noah were alive today he would say, "God is angry that men's and women's desires are impure." I don't have his gift of prophecy, so I can't say what is going to happen, but exactly *what* is going to happen isn't relevant. It's sufficient to know that God wants His people to strive to be holy in thought, desire and heart and to do *everything* we can to obey Him.

If the message of this book ministers to you, please use every means available to bring it to the attention of other Christians. Being an author is only a *small part* of getting any message distributed. You, the reader, can be used by God to change hundreds of people by your efforts to share this message with them.

Exactly *who* needs this message?

1. WIVES

Ladies need to understand that men can be as easily tempted to think immoral thoughts as ladies are tempted to eat excessively. And just as frequently! In some cases, far more frequently. If you find it easy to damage your body by overeating, meditate on how easy it may be for your husband to give in to the temptation of immoral thoughts.

I have been greatly saddened by the many marriages that are ending in divorce as a result of wives becoming overweight. You ladies may react, "That should never be!"

Yes, you would be right, it shouldn't be, but *it is*. Couples who have been together for five, ten and twenty-five years are separated, and the wives are expressing great shock that such a thing could ever happen. I know that on this point I am stepping where angels fear to tread, but please, wives, listen to me. If you permit your love for eating to control your life, you are *inviting* your husband to fasten his attention on another woman. He *should not* do this, but I should give you the facts as they are, so you can then decide what it is that you want most. Once your husband has given his heart to someone else, there may be absolutely *nothing* you can do.

2. HUSBANDS

Men need to understand that ladies need tenderness and understanding. If they don't find these in their husbands, they are tempted to look for them in other men. They can be tempted just as frequently as men are tempted to think immoral thoughts. In some cases, perhaps more frequently. If you find it easy to damage your eternal spirit by thinking immoral thoughts, think how easy it may be for your wife to give in to the temptation of longing for someone else to meet her emotional needs.

You need to be aware that your attitude toward your wife can encourage her to center her attention on another man. Many men have contacted me *after* their wives have filed for divorce, and they were overwhelmed that such a thing could happen. When I studied their problems, it often became clear that the husband failed to provide his wife with the attention, kindness and love she craved. When the husband didn't provide what she needed, she was tempted to look at other men. Of course, she should not have done this, but I should give you the facts as they are, so you can then decide what it is that you want most.

3. UNMARRIED PERSONS

If you believe you should not commit the act of adultery (sex with a married person), or fornication (sex with someone who isn't married), and yet you indulge in lustful thoughts, the odds are that you *will not* be able to be true to what you believe. In fact, the odds are better than nine-to-one that you will eventually slip into some immoral act. The pattern of those who have gone before you has established this tragic record. And the world's environment promises an ever-increasing moral decay.

What is the solution? Accept God's guidelines for His children. Let His Spirit help you to have holy desires. Possible? Yes it is! You can have your mind renewed in the image of Christ. The desire to please God will become stronger than the desire to please your nature.

If, during your period of courtship, you depend on your ability to fight against your desires, you will more than likely become one more example of the nine-to-one odds. But if you seek *holy desires*, you will become an example of what happens when we accept God's will.

Please believe I am suggesting something that is possible. The world has presented sexual desire as being *so strong* that *no one* can control what he desires. Even many Christians have become convinced that if their desires aren't immoral, there must be something wrong with them!

As you seek God's will through His Written Word, His Spirit will actually help you to change your desires! You can face your intended wife or husband, let them look into your eyes, and know they will see the mind of Christ in you.

If you accept God's will in this crucial matter, He will protect you from a multitude of sorrows. If you reject His will, you open yourself to problems as numerous as the grains of sand on the sea shore!

I am not exhorting you to pray for a miracle. I'm informing you of a potential that God has already provided through Jesus. Consider this:

1. God created man with holy desires. Men and women *wanted* to please God. When man sinned, his desires came under the authority of evil forces.

2. Jesus became the second Adam and lived a pure, holy, perfect life. He broke the chains and made it possible for you and me to change *our* desires! Believe that, and you are on the way toward purifying what's on your mind!

And on your way keep in mind:

1. Men have been conditioned to believe that their immoral thoughts are caused by women.

2. Women have been conditioned to believe that their immoral thoughts are caused by men.

Adam said, "The woman...gave me of the tree."

Eve said, "The serpent beguiled me."

Other people *can* lead us into many things, but they can only lead us where we *agree* to go. The ultimate responsibility for *everything* we do rests on no one but ourselves.

The human mind will go to any length to reject guilt. Its objective is to disregard the law of the Creator without suffering the uncomfortable feelings of guilt. You can perhaps verify this from your own experiences. If you have engaged in immoral thinking, you probably have found some way to excuse yourself. The mind says, "I am guilty but..." or "I am not guilty because..."

CHAPTER SIX

THAT PERFECT AFFAIR

Things on planet earth are not usually the way we would like them to be.

We would like to:

Eat what we want and never gain weight

Plant a garden and not get weeds

Give young people good advice and see them follow it

Enjoy living but never get old

Spend money and still have it

Clean the house and have it stay that way

Cook a meal that everyone in the family likes

Change the world for better without having to do anything to make it change.

The world needs to be changed. People need to be changed. We can get ourselves into a position where we know changes need to be made but we don't feel we can do anything. How do we get ourselves into such situations? By trying to mix the wrong things.

A business that had at one time been quite successful, was failing. The owner hired a cost analyst to study the company's methods and personnel and tell him what was wrong.

The analyst's report was short and simple. "Your relatives."

The owner had hired relatives and then felt he couldn't discipline or fire them. They were destroying the company. Even when he knew what the problem was he couldn't bring himself to do what had to be done.

The business man tried to mix his desire to help his family with what would make his business successful. It didn't work. The business failed. The owner lost everything, and his relatives no longer had jobs.

If we try to mix our commitment to Christ with our desire to think immoral thoughts, we have a combination that will not work. God invites us into His family, but He requires that we strive to become like His Son. He always knows in what direction we are moving. Remember the Prodigal Son? When he wanted to leave home, his father helped him. The father gave his son freedom.

God gives us freedom to choose which direction we will take. There is much that needs to be done in this world, but we have the freedom to select what we will do or even to do nothing.

Satanic forces are on the attack. They are committed to the destruction of every Christian element in American life.

Adolph Hitler said he was going to rule Europe. Few paid any attention, much less believed he could accomplish such an impossible task. He believed in himself and eventually ruled most of Europe. The people of other nations enabled Hitler to accomplish his goal — by doing nothing!

Atheistic forces say they are going to strip America of every evidence of Christianity. Will we allow the Holy Spirit to spark a desire in our hearts to be involved in moral issues? That spark was ignited in Jesus when He saw money-changers cheating the people in the Temple. He didn't call for prayer — He moved. The Bible says He was moved with "indignation".

What provokes us to indignation? It usually is something about which we feel deeply. It stirs our emotions. Our hearts tell us we must act. Jesus knew this! That is why He urged us to be pure in heart. If we want to please God, and still indulge in immoral thoughts, we are backed into a corner, just like the business man who couldn't deal with his relatives.

We can see that there are moral problems all around us, but if we have lustful thoughts, we can't rouse ourselves into action. The results can be tragic.

A father longs to spare his sons and daughters the disasters associated with immorality. He wants to tell them to keep their minds free from every thought that might draw them into impure acts. He may love his children so much that he would gladly give his life to protect them. But what if the father lives with lustful thoughts? How can he give his children the information they need if he knows he himself is harboring adulterous thoughts? He can't! And he doesn't. The father doesn't teach his son to think pure thoughts, and that son doesn't teach his sons. Soon the message is lost, and no one remembers that God wants us to be pure in heart.

I see a battle plan for the Body of Christ. We can:

1. Learn God's will for our thoughts.
2. Change our minds to fit His will.
3. Teach our families.
4. Introduce others to the Word of God.
5. Move against evil forces.
6. Elect government officials who will fight for legislation that reflects God's laws.
7. Support those in government who uphold moral principles.

Most of us do not like the idea of being at war. But we are at war. There is no way out. We are either under attack by evil, or attacking evil — advancing or retreating.

There was a time when evil was hidden on the back streets of our nation. Now it flourishes under ten-foot neon signs. It was once confined to sleazy theaters; now television channels it into the living rooms of millions of Americans.

Let's take the situation as it is and make it work for good. We can! You may have been in a church service where all the lights were turned out and one candle was lit.

That one small light could be seen by everyone. Then other candles were lit from that one and the light spread throughout the meeting place.

You and I have the thrill of being a light. Jesus said, "You shine as lights in the midst of a crooked generation." We have the joy of saying to the world, "Jesus has changed my mind. He will change yours too if you will let Him." By sharing the light with the next person, that light will spread in the midst of darkness. But we need to always remember what Jesus said. "If the light that is in you be darkness, how great is that darkness."

I propose that our lights burn brightly. A star may appear the size of a candle's flame yet actually be a million times larger than earth! It looks small because it's so far away. We are not limited in what we can do by our apparent size! We have all the resources of heaven available to assist us!

In the book of Revelation Jesus told the church at Ephesus that He would take the "candle" from their midst *if they were not obedient to God*. We can be obedient. All we need is that spark in our hearts to make whatever changes need to be made.

Consider the atom — too small to be seen. It can move a mountain when its power is released. God sent the Holy Spirit to release power in us. But the Holy Spirit is *holy*. He will only work in a heart that is willing to be used.

You and I have the capacity to bring change into our world. God makes available to each of us more power than we could ever use! The secret is in permitting the Spirit of holiness to work in us.

If your heart longs to be used by God, let Him purify whatever is on your mind.

Jesus said, "If a kingdom be divided against itself, that kingdom cannot stand" (Mark 3:24). Our lives — our kingdoms — are threatened. Our potential losses include our: marriages, homes, children, employment, friends, health and anything else we value.

How do we get into a position where one part of our personality is divided against the other? Here is an illustration of what can happen.

Our legs respond to our brains and carry our bodies from point A to point B.

Introduce alcohol to the brain.

The mind says, "I want to go from A to B."

The brain says, "OK, lets go."

But the "house" has been divided. It isn't capable of fulfilling its function as a unit. Without the brain's help, the legs are unable to move the body.

Our minds may want to protect our marriages, homes and families and to preserve our obedience to God. But if the heart deserts the mind we have a divided kingdom.

You may intend to protect the security of your present lifestyle and eventually to improve it. You do not plan to do anything that is impure or foolish.

During the years that you engaged in impure thoughts, but never followed through on them, your heart increased its desire for an exciting sexual encounter. Your mind successfully held that down.

Then one day you meet a person and something is triggered inside you. *That person* is different and possesses some magical quality that is exactly what you have always wanted. The attraction is so intense that you might easily be convinced that this person was created by God for *you*. You couldn't want them so much if God hadn't given you this intense desire...

If you are fortunate, the other person responds to your advances with, "You must be crazy!"

If you are unfortunate they say, "I feel exactly as you do. We need to get together soon."

All of that magic and harmony and desire promises lasting excitement and fulfillment.

The mind may hesitate and think, What if my husband

finds out? My home would be destroyed. Or, What if her husband finds out? He might kill me.

But the heart will not listen. It has an intense desire to be with *that* person. It refuses to consider fleeing the temptation. Reason and common sense go out the window, and the inner desires rule.

If the temptation is consummated, how long will the magic last? The desires say, "Forever! This is the most real thing that has ever happened to me."

But wait! Jesus said a kingdom divided against itself will fall. If part of you knows that something is wrong and part of you wants it anyhow, the divided kingdom is set up, and the fall will come. Jesus' prediction has been fulfilled tens of thousands of times. Probably millions of people have felt *their* situation was different. Their illicit affairs were too pure to end in tragedy. But the odds are overwhelming. If we get involved in something we know is wrong, our "fall" will come. One wrong step prepares the way for another...and another.

There is only one solution. The desires of our hearts must be changed. We must do whatever is necessary to intensify our desire to please God. He alone knows what will give us lasting pleasure and happiness. We must meditate on His Word regarding thoughts, desires and imaginations. We must keep informing our hearts that pleasing our Creator is our reason for being alive. If we do this, our inner resolve to please God more than self will continue to grow. The kingdom is united in desires, thoughts, goals and ambitions and will remain so until Jesus comes!

Evaluate yourself and ask this question, "Can I commit myself to having the mind of Christ?" You may say to yourself, "That's a nice goal to consider, but I might as well forget it. Some people might be able to have a clean mind, but that's beyond my ability.

Remember two important things:

1. God has said that all His children can, through Christ, do what is right (Phil 4:13). Nothing in your situation makes you ineligible to claim this promise.

70

2. God recognizes our weaknesses, but He never gives up on us. He didn't give up on David. He appointed him King over the strongest nation in the world. David had everything, but his heart desired more. That desire made him a thief and a murderer. If anyone ever gave God a reason to disown a man, it was David. But when David repented, God forgave him. Later, David wrote the Psalms that have helped people for three thousand years. This means that failures do not exclude us from being used of God. He wants you to be successful in your desire to have a pure mind and He will rejoice that you, like David, have the courage to try!

We have a great God. No case is too hard for Him. He doesn't just heal the sick. He also raises the dead! That shows He doesn't look for the easy ways to demonstrate His power.

CHAPTER SEVEN

MY DREAM

My dream was filled with confusion. I knew I had received orders to go back into the Army, but I couldn't find the orders and couldn't remember where I was to report for duty. I was distressed that I couldn't even remember my reporting date.

In the dream there was a crisis when I couldn't find my army clothes. My fatigues and boots were gone. I was going from place to place searching for my uniforms so I could go somewhere, sometime.

When I awakened, it was time to get up, but my shoulder muscles were tight. My face was tense. My hands were pushing down on the bed.

I thought, what a ridiculous dream!

Then I realized that the dream was so intense I must have been expected to learn something. I meditated on all the details, but I couldn't think of one redeeming quality that would make the dream worthwhile.

My mind drifted to several important decisions that I needed to make that day. Each decision could determine the success or failure of important activities. I was straining to decide what I should do.

In the midst of my efforts I was interrupted by a voice within. "That's what your dream was all about."

"What?"

"You are doing now exactly what you were doing in the dream."

"How could that be? In the dream everything centered on completely irrelevant nonsense. Now I'm thinking about things that are important."

"You have only one thing to do today."

By this time I knew there was something the Holy Spirit wanted to teach me.

"Yes, Lord, but what is it I'm supposed to do? There are all these different decisions I must make. What should I do first?"

"Please Me. That is the only thing you have to do."

Then complete silence. I had my orders for the day — for the week — for years to come. The reality of it filled my mind. Pleasing God was what I had to do! Everything else was secondary. My concern over the decisions I needed to make was as unnecessary as locating my army clothes in the dream.

All that day the message from God filled my mind. My mission, my work, my whole duty was to please God. Each time I felt tension in my shoulder muscles or face, I remembered the dream, and peace flowed through my mind. God was working to change my understanding of what was important to Him. I wanted to be used by God to change the world — He wanted to change me.

Romans 8:29 says, "...to be conformed to the image of His Son." This is what God wanted to do in me. His Son knew what His purpose was on this earth. Redeem the human race? Heal the sick? Provide salvation? Be crucified and resurrected? He did all these things, but they weren't His only mission. His total mission was to please God.

If I picture Jesus as only a man, just like any other man, I would see Him as powerless. If I picture Jesus as so separated from mankind that He has nothing in common with us, how can I use Him as my example?

I see Jesus as One I can look to as a perfect model. He was pure, but He permitted Himself to suffer every temptation that we do.

He was tempted to have wrong thoughts, but He never had them! Some may react unfavorably to the idea that Jesus was tempted to think immoral thoughts. But He was tempted in all points as we are. The difference is in His reaction! He was tempted to be discouraged, but was never discouraged. We can read "conformed to the image of His Son" and know that there is a comparison between the temptations He endured and our own. When we remember our own failures we may think, I could never be sinless in my desires so why should I try? But He endured the same temptations so He *could be* our example!

Satan released maximum temptation on Jesus at one point in His life. Satan became so desperate that he offered to release all the influence he had over every part of this world. He was determined! "Just fall down and worship me once, Jesus, for only one second, and everything I have will be yours."

Since Satan went this far, what previous offers must he have given Jesus? Whatever they were, nothing succeeded. Jesus remained our perfect example.

The point is, no matter what temptations Jesus faced, His mind remained pure.

You and I can be changed once we perceive an image of ourselves made into His likeness. He was human enough to serve as our example, yet divine enough to be a perfect sacrifice. His death and resurrection released the power that we need to follow Him.

I do not believe that the moment a man accepts Jesus as Saviour he is expected to be immediately pure in heart! It doesn't happen that way. Neither do I believe that God assigns an angel to clobber a new Christian if he or she slips into a pattern of wrong thinking.

Before we became Christians, our minds were filled with wrong thoughts. Our memories and inclinations reflected our less-than-perfect natures. At our new birth, by the grace of God, we may have been instantly delivered of some bad habits, but others clung to our coat-tails waiting for an opportunity to control our future.

I've experienced and observed God's great patience. He loves, forgives and cares for us. He longs for us to mature and lay aside things that hold us back.

Why doesn't He make us instantly free of all temptations? This little dot of time in eternity is our brief opportunity to learn how to be obedient to God when everything around us says, "Disobey!"

When we are received into God's family, we may be as weak as a new-born eagle. We have great potential, but as we develop, we need considerable understanding and care.

The skeptic might think a new Christian is a fraud if he sees in him anything less than perfection. Those who know nothing about an eaglet might think he should know how to fly — but he doesn't.

When a man or woman has been a Christian for months or even years, he still has many faults, and may be considered a hypocrite by the skeptic. An eagle can be mature enough to have wings capable of lifting him to the heavens, but that doesn't mean he can fly! A novice might say, "Shove him out of the nest and he will learn to fly before he hits the ground." But he won't! Eagles don't learn to fly that way. Push him out of the nest too soon and he will fall like a rock and land on his head.

Day after day the mother eagle perches on the edge of the nest and patiently flaps her wings. The young eagle watches and eventually imitates his instructor. Flap, flap. "Hey, this is fun, but why are we doing it?"

By and by the long wings develop muscles. At the right time the giant mother nudges the fearful offspring out into the world. The mother flaps her wings like she has done so often before, and the babe follows her example. Together they now reach up into the sky.

The new Christian may want to "fly", but he often doesn't want to go to all the work it takes to develop spiritual muscles.

God knows our potential, and He keeps reminding us of who we are. We feel it when the spirit within says, "Those thoughts you are having aren't right. You need to change."

"But I can't change!"

"Yes you can. Look around you. See the world I have created. It is glorious. Behold the heavens. They tell you of my glory. Look at a flower — it reflects my love for beauty. I made you for purity and goodness. You can do it!"

Paul wrote, "We are making every thought captive to the obedience of Christ" (II Cor 10:5 N.A.S.). He was giving us an up-to-date report on what the early church was learning.

The Greeks of Corinth lived pretty much as slaves under the Roman Empire. They understood steel and swords and soldiers controlling everything. Paul is describing a new brand of captive — one held by the love of Jesus. In verse one he said, "I beseech you by the meekness and gentleness of Christ."

The Christians of Corinth faced no easy task in their efforts to have the mind of Christ. It was customary in Corinth to offer public prayers asking the gods to multiply their prostitutes! The religious leaders bound themselves, by vows, to increase the number of such women, for this occupation was considered spiritually uplifting. To people with this background Paul was presenting his challenge for purity in every thought!

Releasing our minds to Christ's control must be a voluntary act. He will not accept authority over our thoughts unless this is what *we* want. Jesus is not pressuring us to make our thoughts like His! Rather, He is saying, "You were polluted by thoughts that enslaved you. I say that you can be free."

Like the baby eagle, we need to stretch our wings and feel what it's like to be created in God's image. We were made for lofty heights, where the air is fresh and clean. He gives us His Spirit to convince us that we are worthy of reaching for the goal of holiness in heart and mind.

We may not soar into realms of perfection while we are still here in this flesh, but we can at least begin to flap our wings and declare our freedom in Christ. We do not have to be bound by the beggarly thoughts of impure desires! God has declared that we have the capacity to be changed into the image of His Son!

Like the baby eagle, you and I received our new lives way up in high places. We were born for heavenly adventures. The spirit within us longs for everything that is holy. Haven't you felt that longing many times?

Our flesh wants to stay down in the baser environment. It relishes the earth-bound desires that seem so enjoyable, but have proven to be so futile.

We are free to fly. Jesus is our example. He said we could follow Him. When we first try, it seems impossible. Our minds may say, "I can't. I'm too human." We *are* woefully human, but because of Jesus we can change. He provides the way.

What's on *your* mind? Does it need to change? If so, begin to move out and up. Leave the impure thoughts behind. We are spiritual beings. We are born to attain spiritual heights.

And now to the ultimate solution:

GOD'S WRITTEN WORD

ATTENTION!

You may have decided that you agree with my message but are not overly interested in studying additional Scriptures.

CAUTION!

I believe the Holy Spirit has given me extra help in understanding the following references. My comments are brief but crucial.

BE ALERT!

Be alert to the human tendency to merely scan the Scriptures on the following pages. If what I have written thus far has pointed out spiritual needs in your life, please believe that you need to *carefully study* Chapter Eight.

Perhaps you may not initially understand the need for including so many Scriptures in this chapter. But please believe me! Stories about other people's lives are interesting, but they do not have the power to change our hearts. The human desire for immoral thoughts is so strong that only God's Word can change us.

Saturate your mind with the Bible verses in this book and you will maintain a mind that is free. With a clean mind, the door is wide open for you to enter into a multitude of blessings from God.

CHAPTER EIGHT

THE ULTIMATE SOLUTION

There are those who teach that all we have to do is believe the promises in the Bible and we can have anything we want. God's promises are true, but if we disregard His will, we cannot convince Him to give us the things we want. His promises are based upon our obedience. This is made quite emphatic in:

1. Psalm 66:18 "If I regard iniquity in my heart, the Lord will not hear me:"

2. Proverbs 1:25 "You have ignored all my counsel...27 When distress and anguish come upon you, (RSV) 28 Then shall they call upon me, but I will not answer; they shall seek me early, but they shall not find me:

We will do well to be obedient. None of us can perfectly obey, and He hasn't demanded that we be perfect. But He warns against "ignoring" His counsel. If we choose to ignore His hatred of immorality, then we should not expect Him to respond to our prayers.

3. I John 3:22 "And whatsoever we ask, we receive of him, because we keep his commandments and do those things that are pleasing in his sight."

And now to the focal point of my message — the formula for becoming what God wants us to be.

Please examine the following Scriptures thoughtfully! If we meditate on these verses, we can be victorious in our search for clean thoughts and desires. My purpose in writing this book is to present a prescription for victory! Every person needs to understand that *God's purpose* in everything He has said is to help us.

There are hundreds of verses that I have not included. I wanted to give you enough to demonstrate God's attention to this subject and yet not so many that you would be kept from carefully considering each verse.

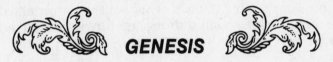

GENESIS

1:1 In the beginning God created...

There is enough in these five words to produce a lifetime of clean thoughts. Every person we see is His creation! When I see an attractive lady I have learned to respond with, "Thank You Lord for that beautiful creation!" My praise causes joy to rise in my heart. I would be delighted for the lady to know the thoughts of my heart for they have already been blessed by God.

> *6:5 And God saw that the wickedness of man was great in the earth, and that every IMAGIN-ATION of the THOUGHTS of his heart was only evil continually. 6 And it repented the Lord that he had made man on the earth, and it grieved him at his heart.*

Evil imaginations and evil thoughts in men's minds caused God to wish He had never created mankind. These verses — alone — are sufficient reasons for us to carefully guard our thoughts.

EXODUS

20:14 Thou shalt not commit adultery.

Like any loving parent, God uses His goodness to draw us to repentance. If that fails, then He often administers the corrective action necessary to get our attention.

20:17 Thou shalt not covet thy neighbor's... wife.

This is much stronger than saying, "Thou shalt not *take* thy neighbor's wife." God is saying we are not permitted to *want to have her*. Only a *strong* desire to please God can control even what we *want* to have.

LEVITICUS

In the Old Testament God makes severe judgments against immorality. Most of us would prefer to flee to the God of grace as revealed in the New Testament. But it is important that we refresh our minds as to how God feels about His moral laws. Once we have a clear picture of this, we are much better prepared to understand why He wants our thoughts to be pure.

20:1 The Lord spake unto Moses saying...7 Sanctify yourselves therefore, and be ye holy: for I am the Lord your God. 10 The man that committeth adultery with another man's wife, even he that committeth adultery with his neighbor's wife, the adulterer and the adulteress shall surely be put to death.

NUMBERS

One of the children of Israel brought a foreign woman into the Jewish camp and led her to his tent.

> *25:7 When Phinehas...saw it, he rose up from among the congregation, and took a javelin in his hand; 8 And he went after the man of Israel into the tent, and thrust both of them through, the man of Israel, and the woman through her belly. So the plague was stayed from the children of Israel. 10 And the Lord spake unto Moses, saying, 11 Phinehas...hath turned my wrath away from the children of Israel, while he was zealous for my sake among them that I consumed not the children of Israel in my jealousy.*

This passage gives us a dramatic picture of how God feels when his laws are disobeyed. If Phinehas had not used corrective action, God would have taken many lives. We may often need to take swift, corrective action regarding out thoughts and imaginations. In some Christians' minds, immoral thoughts have been permitted to have free reign. This book is an effort to help combat the tide of immorality that is crashing against the hearts and minds of Christian men and women. Some groups are warning us against x-rated movies and pornography, but I believe we will accomplish much more if we first cleanse our own hearts and then unite to change the world around us.

In my lifetime I have heard many sermons on the need for Christians to become "holy". But the emphasis was nearly always on outward actions. Don't do this or don't do that. Should we spend an entire lifetime trying to avoid doing wrong, while something within us continually *desires* to do wrong? The exciting thing is that the Bible contains the help we need to have desires that *will be* pleasing to God.

DEUTERONOMY

5:29 Oh that there were such an HEART in them that they would fear me, and keep all my commandments always that it might be well with them, and with their children forever.

God's desire has not changed and His promises are still in force. If we can bring our hearts into harmony with His will, He says everything will go well for us and even for our children. What a blessed promise!

JUDGES

2:14 The anger of the Lord was hot against Israel, and he delivered them into the hands of spoilers that spoiled them, and he sold them into the hands of their enemies round about, so that they could not any longer stand before their enemies.

What caused God's anger toward Israel?

2:12 They followed other gods. 13 They forsook the Lord.

Immorality is a "god" that we must be careful never to follow. Israel was God's "chosen people", yet their enemies overcame them when they disobeyed Him.

Keep Moving Forward!

RUTH

3:11 All the city of my people doth know that thou art a virtuous woman.

An entire book of the Bible, set apart to honor a virtuous woman! What a blessing and what an incentive to all of us. If we want God to bless our homes, our families, our work and our health, we should honor His love of virtue.

I SAMUEL

12:24 Fear the Lord, and serve him in truth with all your HEART: for consider how great things he hath done for you.

God's plan of salvation is kind and full of grace. But we can receive the gift of eternal life and still be sadly imperfect. God asks us to consider His goodness and then serve Him with *all our hearts*. We can reject His plea and continue to think whatever thoughts we desire. If we do this, there may be serious consequences. We never know what they might be. It seems to me that often evil forces themselves decide what the consequences will be! This is a painful way to learn — obedience is far easier!

II SAMUEL

11:2 And it came to pass in an eveningtide, that David arose from off his bed, and walked upon the roof of the king's house: and from the roof he saw a woman washing herself; and the woman was very beautiful to look upon. 3 And David sent and enquired after the woman.

David looked...and wanted...and so began his tragic downfall. Men, consider this carefully. David probably didn't think he was capable of doing the things he eventually did. The problem, of course, was not that he happened to see Bathsheba, but that he did not control his thoughts.

I KINGS

11:1 King Solomon loved many strange women ...4 It came to pass, when Solomon was old, that his wives turned away his HEART after other gods.

If we persist in our desire to have wrong thoughts, our hearts will be turned away from God. It will happen slowly and so subtly that we may not recognize what is happening. Even Solomon, the wisest man who ever lived, didn't realize that his heart was being turned away from God.

Keep Scriptures on Your Mind!

I CHRONICLES

16:29 Give unto the Lord the glory due unto his name: bring an offering, and come before him. Worship the Lord in the beauty of holiness.

Two of the most acceptable offerings we can bring to God are clean hearts and minds. These offerings can be brought to Him by anyone — the poorest of men, those in prisons and those confined to their beds. No service to God, no matter how great or well-known, could possibly compare with the service of a heart that reflects the beauty of His holiness. None of us are perfect, but *He knows* when we do our best to let His Spirit control our thoughts. The great tragedy is that many Christian men and women know their thoughts are not right, yet they make no serious effort to change.

29:1 David the king said unto all the congregation....3 I have set my affection to the house of my God. 9 Then the people rejoiced, for that they offered willingly, because with perfect heart they offered willingly to the Lord.

When we are fully persuaded that God is making human beings His home, we begin to honor that home as His. We give that honor willingly and joyfully.

EZRA

7:23 Whatsoever is commanded by the God of heaven, let it be diligently done for the house of the God of heaven.

God has repeatedly emphasized that His house is to be treated with great care. Now God makes His house in the hearts of all who accept His Son as Saviour. If we receive the benefits of salvation through Christ, we must accept the responsibilities of caring for God's dwelling place. He has repeatedly told us that the thoughts and desires of our minds must be appropriate for *His dwelling place*.

9:6 Oh my God, I am ashamed and blush to lift up my face to thee, my God: for our iniquities are increased over our head and our trespass is grown up unto the heavens.

The people of Israel saw the men and women of the heathen nations and wanted them. Ezra was ashamed of what he saw. As Christians we should be deeply ashamed of what is going on today. Immorality flourishes.

ESTHER

1:10 When the heart of the king was merry with wine he commanded...the chamberlains 11 To bring Vashti the queen...to shew the people and the princes her beauty: for she was fair to look on. 12 But the queen Vashti refused to come... Therefore was the king very wroth, and his anger burned in him.

Men have accepted the idea that if a woman is beautiful in her outward appearance, she can meet their desires and needs. This has proven to be false, but men continue to believe it. The handsome, dashing man can likewise bring great suffering into a woman's life.

JOB

24:15 The eye of the adulterer waiteth for the twilight saying, No eye shall see me: and disguiseth his face. 18...their portion is cursed in the earth.

What is the "portion" that could come under God's curse? It could be our portion of *anything*! It might be the health of our families or our finances. This certainly *does not* mean that every time we have trouble that God has placed a curse on part of our lives! Too often, God is portrayed only as a God of love. His love is far greater than we will ever realize, but His judgments are also clearly a part of His nature. We need to recognize this.

*10:1 Why standest thou afar off, O Lord? Why
hidest thou thyself in times of trouble?*

If our thoughts are unclean, God may seem to be "afar
off" when we pray. In times of trouble we may cry for help
and it will seem that He doesn't hear us.

*10:4 The wicked...will not seek after God: God
is not in all his THOUGHTS.*

God wants to have a part in all our thoughts.

*14:2 The Lord looked down from heaven upon
the children of men, to see if there were any that
did understand, and seek God. 3 They are all
gone aside, they are all together become filthy
(impure): there is none that doeth good, no, not
one.*

It must have broken God's heart to say something as
strong as this. He is still looking for those who "understand". I, for one, have been slow to learn.

*19:14 Let the words of my mouth and the MED-
ITATION of my heart, be acceptable in thy
sight, O Lord, my strength, and my redeemer.*

Our meditation *is* important if we want His strength to
work for us.

23:1 The Lord is my shepherd; I shall not want.

Exciting sermons can be preached on this verse but some have placed all the emphasis on "I shall not want". The emphasis being, that if we claim Jesus as our Saviour, we will never want for anything. It is then pointed out that we do not need to lack health, wealth, success, popularity or any good thing. I know this kind of teaching is warmly welcomed. Everyone likes to be part of something that promises so much.

The psalmist first said that the Lord *was his Shepherd.* To him that meant that he was following the Lord as a sheep follows the shepherd. As a result, he knew he would never be in need. What most of us want, is to be able to *do* what we want and still *have* what we want. In other words, we want the blessings of following Jesus *without* having to obey Him.

It was common procedure in David's time for a shepherd to discipline a sheep that would not follow. Often that discipline was to break one of the sheep's legs. Then, when it could not walk, the shepherd would carry it in his arms. By the time the bone was mended, the sheep would be so attached to the shepherd, that it would stay close by his side for the rest of its life.

It is harmful to think we can always obtain what we want from God and still do things that He has forbidden. God always chastens those He loves for their own good. He knows that as a sheep needs to be close to the shepherd for protection, we need to stay where our Shepherd can watch over us. Otherwise, we too will be consumed by the wolves.

*24:3 Who shall ascend into the hill of the Lord?
or who shall stand in his holy place? He that
hath clean hands, and a pure heart.*

Any efforts to come into His "holy place" will fail if we do not strive to have a pure heart.

In a very real sense, any Christian can come into God's presence. Our sins do not cause a complete separation. Thank the Lord! But sins of any kind can prevent close fellowship with God and may hinder answers to prayer.

Jesus said He and the Father were always in close communion — not because He was the Son, but because, "I do always those things that please him" (John 8:29).

Jesus made a distinction between "disciples" and those who were *indeed* His disciples. He said, "If ye continue in my word, then are ye my disciples indeed" (John 8:31). What a blessing it would be if Jesus should ever look at one of us and say, "This is indeed my disciple"!

*139:23 Search me, O God, and know my heart:
try me, and know my THOUGHTS: 24 And see
if there be any wicked way in me.*

Now is a good time to repeat this verse as a prayer.

PROVERBS

1:10 My son, if sinners entice thee, consent thou not.

Members of the opposite sex often "entice" us.

4:14 Enter not into the path of the wicked, and go not in the way of evil men.

Evil men say that their way of life is more gratifying and fulfilling than God's way. If we examine their lives, it becomes evident that their personal lives are anything but happy.

5:3 The lips of a strange woman drop as an honeycomb, and her mouth is smoother than oil: 4 But her end is bitter as wormwood, sharp as a two-edged sword.

Our *flesh* often longs for the things that our *spirits* know will bring trouble. God is warning us that often things that look sweet as honey may prove to be bitter.

> *6:23 The commandment is a lamp; and the law is light; and reproofs of instruction are the way of life: 24 To keep thee from the evil woman, from the flattery of the tongue of a strange woman. 25 Lust not after her beauty in thine HEART; neither let her take thee with her eyelids. 26 For by means of a whorish woman a man is brought to a piece of bread: and the adulteress will hunt for the precious life. 27 Can a man take fire in his bosom, and his clothes not be burned?*

How many men have heard the above words read, yet have been "burned"?

Men and women are reluctant to accept the fact that wrong thoughts — all too often — lead to overt acts.

> *6:32 Whoso committeth adultery with a woman lacketh understanding: he that doeth it destroyeth his own soul. 33 A wound and dishonor shall he get; and his reproach shall not be wiped away.*

Our soul is a precious gift from God that can be destroyed. It is sensitive to God's words, and we can preserve its health by doing those things that He has blessed.

12:5 The THOUGHTS of the righteous are right.

We have the opportunity to bring our thoughts into harmony with God's will.

15:15 He that is of a merry heart hath a continual feast.

Once we begin the process of permitting God's Word to purify our "hearts" then the heart becomes "merry". Life takes on new joy.

As I removed from my mind the thoughts that were immoral, I noticed a change. Sometimes as I walked along a street I would suddenly feel excited. Somewhere within I felt new joy bubbling up. I frequently wanted to shout, "Oh God, I'm so happy."

15:26 The THOUGHTS of the wicked are an abomination to the Lord.

Knowing and understanding this is an excellent motivation to have pure thoughts.

21:10 The soul of the wicked DESIRETH evil.

Notice the emphasis God places on "desires". He wants our desires to be right. This is a high calling.

23:6 Eat thou not the bread (Don't have fellowship with) of him that hath an evil eye. 7 For as he THINKETH in his heart, so is he.

You may think, I have wrong thoughts in my mind, but of course I would never do the things I'm thinking. God says that as we *think* so we *are*! He evaluates our thoughts as a very real part of the person we *are*.

24:9 The THOUGHT of foolishness is sin.

Sometimes, men's impure thoughts are absurd. They may imagine themselves having relationships with people such as movie stars and magazine cover girls. They know the experience will never happen, and may feel they are not hurting anyone. God classifies such use of our minds as foolishness.

ECCLESIASTES

2:9 I was great and increased more than all that were before me in Jerusalem...10 And whatsoever mine eyes desired I kept not from them, I withheld not my heart from any joy...11 And, behold, all was vanity and vexation of spirit, and there was no profit under the sun.

What an abundance he must have had!

Someone may say, "If only I could have that woman, (or that man) I would be happy." But achieving such desires often brings vexation to our spirits.

Some may think that as a man or woman gets older the temptation to have wrong things on their minds decreases. But sometimes the reverse is true. As a person gets older he often thinks life is passing him by.

"All is vanity..." Nothing on this earth holds the key to satisfaction. Jesus said, "I am the way".

Some experiences contribute to a feeling of happiness, but feelings change, perhaps leaving us more unhappy than before. God advises us to seek His will first. Then He will take care of our desires for satisfaction. He has demonstrated this to me so many times that I'm gradually learning to believe Him.

SONG OF SOLOMON

8:7 If a man should offer for love all the wealth of his house, it would be scornfully refused (MLB).

Inside each of us there is a need for love that cannot be met with material possessions nor sex. I have talked with many men who frequented houses of ill-repute. They often reported a feeling of disgust with themselves when they left the establishment.

Immoral relationships between those who are seeking genuine love, and feel they *do* love one another, invariably lead to resentment, stress and often deep bitterness. When God created our capacity to love, He united it with our obedience to His will. If we ignore His will, the beautiful attribute of love will be changed into baser emotions.

ISAIAH

55:7 Let the wicked forsake his way, and the unrighteous man his THOUGHTS...for he will abundantly pardon.

Some have not yet heard that their thoughts could be made clean. I want to help Christians learn the great potential we have in Christ. As we are changed we can help bring a cleansing to our nation.

55:8 For my THOUGHTS are not your THOUGHTS, neither are your ways my ways, saith the Lord.

We may not understand why God is so interested in the secret parts of our minds, but He wants *our thoughts* to be in harmony with *His*.

59:2 Your sins have hid his face from you. 7 Their THOUGHTS are THOUGHTS of iniquity.

Our thoughts are able to separate us from God. How I wish I had known this years ago!

JEREMIAH

4:14 How long shall thy vain THOUGHTS lodge within thee?

Ask yourself, "How long will I permit bad thoughts to lodge in my heart?" Thoughts "lodge within" as long as we welcome them.

6:19 Hear, O earth: behold, I will bring evil upon this people, even the fruit of their THOUGHTS, because they have not hearkened unto my words.

God has promised that we will receive the fruits of our thoughts. He keeps His word.

LAMENTATIONS

1:8 Jerusalem hath grievously sinned; therefore she is removed: all that honored her despise her, because they have seen her nakedness.

When God wants to describe a vile situation, He refers to it as a woman whose clothes have been removed, causing her to stand naked. If a man mentally disrobes a woman, in God's eyes he is shaming her!

> *8:12 Then said he unto me, Son of man, hast thou seen what the ancients of the house of Israel do in the dark, every man in the chambers of his IMAGERY? For they say, The Lord seeth us not.*

If we feel a need to keep our imaginations secret, then we want to keep them "in the dark".

> *11:5 And the Spirit of the Lord fell upon me, and said unto me, Speak; Thus saith the Lord...I know the things that come into your MIND, every one of them.*

Pause...Meditate on God's careful attention to what is on our minds.

> *16:29 Thou hast multiplied thy fornication...30 How weak is thine HEART, saith the Lord God, seeing thou doest all these things.*

In our hearts — where our desires live — dwell the decisions that we will make tomorrow.

> *22:30 I sought for a man among them, that should make up the hedge, and stand in the gap before me for the land, that I should not destroy it.*

There is a great need today for Christians who will "stand in the gap" before God, lest He destroy our land. We can protect our families from destruction by cleansing our thoughts.

> *33:31 With their mouth they shew much love, but their heart goeth after their covetousness.*

It may be difficult to understand why God is so against covetousness. We may think, I don't intend to *take* something that isn't mine. What harm can it do if I simply *want* it?

There are principles involved that God understands better than we do. For example, Satan *wanted* God's throne and caused great havoc in heaven. Satan *wanted* to rule the earth and used his power to corrupt mankind. Eve *wanted* God's knowledge and disobeyed God.

When man wants something that isn't his, the odds are great that one day he will reach out and *take* it. God has made known His will. "If it isn't yours, don't permit your heart to wish for that which belongs to another."

DANIEL

When referring to the end times, Daniel wrote:

12:10 Many shall be purified, and made white.

God promises that as the end of this world draws near many of His children will be purified. Even as you read this book, the Spirit is calling you to be pure and clean in thought. God promised this, and you and I are privileged to share in the fulfillment of His promise.

HOSEA

4:12 The spirit of whoredoms hath caused them to err.

There is a spirit that influences men and women to entertain bad thoughts. It is a powerful force. Its ultimate aim is to combat God's will for His people. Once we come under this influence, it may be difficult to gain our freedom. But Jesus gives each of us the strength we need to declare our deliverance.

JOEL

2:27 My people shall never be ashamed. 28 And it shall come to pass afterward, that I will pour out my spirit upon all flesh. 30 And I will shew wonders in the heavens and in the earth.

If we have reason to "be ashamed" of what is in the secret parts of our minds, we have reason to seek the help of the Holy Spirit.

Part of the preparation for the last days, with its "signs and wonders", includes God's people being *changed* by His Spirit.

AMOS

5:15 Hate the evil, and love the good.

Unfortunately, some Christians think immoral thoughts and do not consider them evil. The issue is side-stepped, swept under the carpet, left to reside in peace.

OBADIAH

1:3 The pride of thine heart hath deceived thee.

It is easy to permit old habits to control our lives. If we are deceived by our *own hearts* it is often difficult for anyone to convince us that we need to change!

JONAH

1:2 Go to Nineveh...and cry against it; for their wickedness is come up before me.

Disobedience comes to God's attention.

NAHUM

1:2 God is jealous...6 Who can stand before his indignation? 9 What do ye IMAGINE against the Lord?

"God is jealous." It is dangerous to misuse what He has created. Throughout Scripture God repeatedly emphasizes misuse of sex as being especially offensive to Him. Through proper use of sex, man participates in the divine act of creation. This experience is so sacred that God demands compliance with His will. Perhaps this is why He considers homosexuality so repulsive. In the Old Testament He slaughtered every man, woman and child in cities that openly practiced homosexuality. His Word says He gets "furious".

HABAKKUK

2:9 Woe to him that coveteth.

We must *never* covet. His rule is not subject to change.

ZEPHANIAH

2:3 Seek righteousness...it may be ye shall be hid in the day of the Lord's anger.

Scientific wonders make it possible for immorality to spread world-wide. Side-by-side march scientific advancements that can create violent destruction. God may soon permit these forces to be unleashed. Now, more than at any other time in history, it is important for us to "seek righteousness".

3:1 Woe to her that is filthy and polluted.

We can determine whether our thoughts are "polluted". If we act-out sexual immorality in our imaginations, we are polluted in God's eyes.

A little child questions why adults make such a big thing out of dirty clothes. Christians who do not want to change, may not understand why *God* makes such a big thing out of immoral thoughts.

Stimulate Your Interest!

HAGGAI

1:6 Ye have sown much and bring in little; ye eat, but ye have not enough; ye drink, but ye are not filled with drink; ye clothe you but there is none warm; and he that earneth wages earneth wages to put it into bags with holes.

This verse covers a multitude of problems! Working and not seeming to accomplish anything. Eating and not feeling satisfied. Drinking but always wanting more. Having clothes but always feeling there is "nothing to wear". Earning money but seeing it disappear. What causes these problems? God says, "Consider your ways."

END OF OLD TESTAMENT SCRIPTURES

MATTHEW

5:8 Blessed are the pure in heart.

Thoughts, desires and imaginations originate in our hearts and therefore represent the quality of purity that is within.

6:23 If thine eye be evil, thy whole body shall be full of darkness.

Our eyes reflect the desires of our hearts. If we use our eyes to stimulate evil thoughts, we are placing our whole body in spiritual darkness.

22:37 Thou shalt love the Lord thy God with all thy heart, and with all thy soul and with ALL THY MIND. 38 This is the first and great commandment.

Please remember the high priority God has given to what happens in our minds.

God is clear and explicit regarding His will for the human mind. If we entertain adulterous thoughts we do not love Him with all our minds.

23:27...Ye are like unto whited (white-washed) sepulchres, which indeed appear beautiful outward, but are within full of dead men's bones, and of all uncleanness. (Not morally pure) 28 Even so ye also outwardly appear righteous unto men, but within ye are full of hypocrisy and iniquity (impurity).

To what lengths are we willing to go in order to "appear righteous unto men"? Most of us have a strong desire to appear to others as honest, reliable and trustworthy. Our reputation is a valuable asset. But Jesus is saying we should be more concerned with what is within our hearts. If everyone we know could see our every thought, what would they think of us?

MARK

4:19 The lusts of other things...choke the word, and it becometh unfruitful.

If we persist in coveting, our spiritual lives can be choked.

LUKE

12:2 There is nothing covered, that shall not be revealed, neither hid, that shall not be known.

The thoughts we now have in secret will one day be known to all. This is one of God's "promises".

16:15 God knoweth your HEARTS: for that which is highly esteemed among men is abomination in the sight of God.

Our outward appearances can have every characteristic of goodness, but God looks on the heart.

24:38 And he (Jesus) said unto them, why are ye troubled? and why do THOUGHTS arise in your hearts?

Thoughts of any kind come from our hearts and Jesus considers us responsible.

JOHN

3:20 For every one that doeth evil hateth the light, neither cometh to the light, lest his deeds should be reproved.

Those who think immoral thoughts would not want their families or friends to know what they were thinking, lest their "deeds should be reproved".

3:21 But he that doeth truth cometh to the light, that his deeds may be made manifest, that they are wrought in God.

This person would be perfectly at ease if his thoughts were pictured on a screen above his head, for he has already considered that *God* observes what he thinks.

4:23 The hour cometh, and now is, when the true worshiper shall worship the Father in spirit and in truth: for the Father seeketh such to worship him.

To understand this verse we need to remember what Jesus was discussing. He told the woman at the well that she had had five husbands and was now living with another man. This text indicates that God wants us to worship Him with a morally uncontaminated spirit.

I believe the Holy Spirit is today renewing the same message.

8:34 Jesus answered them, Verily, verily I say unto you, Whosoever committeth sin is the servant of sin.

If we are bound by the habits of wrong thinking, we lose control of many parts of our lives. Our spiritual life is greatly weakened. Our ability to understand Scripture can be greatly limited. Our relationships with other people can suffer. In other words, we are the "servants of sin".

8:36 If the Son therefore shall make you free, ye shall be free indeed.

If you have bad habits that you cannot break, please understand that you are not living in the victory that God wants. It could be that immoral thoughts are so weakening your mind that you aren't able to exert will-power.

Millions of people are looking for a new way to lose weight. They may have tried every available diet, yet they are continually tormented by their "inability" to control what they eat. When they "control" their intake by under-eating, they become so irritable and grumpy that they aren't fit to live with. Their morale drops so low that they finally decide to go back to eating whatever they want. This is no way to live! I am in no way implying that persons who are overweight have problems with immoral thinking! I *am* saying that Jesus came to give us freedom to control what we think and what we want! This may be a delightful surprise to you. If it is, begin taking charge of your thoughts.

If you are unhappy about *anything*, please believe that it is God's plan for you to be at peace. You don't have to be a super Christian to receive His help, but you do have to be willing to accept His will. Remember that Jesus said His yoke is easy and His burden is light. It is Satan's yoke that is tough to bear!

111

14:1 Let not your heart be troubled.

Christians often endure great agony because of something others are or are not doing. The Christian tells himself over and over that he will not let that person bother him anymore. He means it and intends to be victorious over the situation. But before he knows what is happening, he is back to worrying or being upset. If he examines his thought life, he may see that he has not yet permitted Christ to make him "free indeed".

Consider carefully how exciting it could be to permit Jesus to give you greater control over your thoughts! Many people spend endless hours worrying about one thing or another. They know that their worries are destroying their health and happiness, but they don't have the will-power to stop. I'm sharing with you an exciting truth that can change your life.

We have been conditioned to believe that if a husband leaves his wife, or vice versa, life is then supposed to be miserable for the rejected mate. What Christians often fail to realize is that Jesus can set us free from the heartaches others give us. We may weep for a season, but through Him we can be ushered into peace.

And because of Jesus, even death is swallowed up in victory! We can lose a loved one in death and eventually be victorious! This is real victory! Mary and I learned this not too long ago in the accidental death of our oldest son.

As parents we need to know that it is God's will for us to release our children to Him. It is not His will for us to live in continued grief and sorrow when they come into hard places. It is only natural for parents to grieve when their children suffer, but when we release our children to Him, He wants us to believe He is working in their lives for *their good*. We need to remember that God resurrected His own Son from the grave and that He wants us to trust Him to care for *our* children.

A Christian's heart can quickly become "troubled" if he opens his mind to lustful thoughts. That one "trouble" then acts as a magnet to pick up others. Jesus knows that our bodies and minds were not designed by God to carry troubles. If we insist on carrying them, we suffer many things. If we get caught in a cycle of troubles, we always think we are helpless. The truth of the matter is we are *never* helpless. Jesus would not have told us to "never be troubled" if He thought He was giving us an impossible assignment.

> *17:17 Make them pure and holy through teaching them your words of truth. 19 And I consecrate myself to meet their need for growth in truth and holiness (TLB).*

If we realize what our failures are and spend all our lives feeling guilty, our guilt will *never* help us. If we live in fear because of our sins or failures, our fear will never help us. Jesus is saying that His words have the strength to change us. We need changing, but our condition isn't hopeless!

Jesus consecrated Himself to meet our need whatever it might be! This is a sufficient guarantee to cause each one of us to believe He has a solution for our situation.

> *6:26 "Verily, verily, I say unto you, Ye seek me, not because ye saw the miracles, but because ye did eat of the loaves, and were filled."*

This means we *are* able to get our priorities mixed up! If we cooperate with the Holy Spirit's efforts to make us "pure in heart", He will take care of other matters. He knows we have material needs, but He wants us to seek Him rather than His miracles.

ACTS

8:21 Thy heart is not right in the sight of God. 22 Repent therefore of this thy wickedness, and pray God, if perhaps the THOUGHT of thine heart may be forgiven thee.

We are responsible for whatever comes from our hearts.

ROMANS

1:21 When they knew God, they glorified him not as God.

What does the Holy Spirit mean when He says people "knew God" but then did not glorify Him "as God"? He immediately clarifies this. He is referring to those who become disobedient to God in the use of their imaginations! They "became vain in their imaginations, and their foolish heart was darkened". Verses 24-29 make it clear that these disobedient imaginations include dishonoring the human body (Not respecting another person's body as the temple of God).

1:24 Because men are such fools, God has given them over to do the filthy things their hearts desire (GN).

It is extremely important that we "desire" the right things!

25...They worship and serve what God has created instead of the Creator himself (GN).

A strong statement!

2:16 God shall judge the secrets of men.

If we have anything on our minds that we want to keep secret, those thoughts are scheduled to be judged.

6:12 Let not sin therefore reign in your mortal bodies, to make you obey their passions. 13 Do not yield your members to sin as instruments of wickedness.

If we yield our minds to unclean thoughts, we need to be reminded that God wants that member to be holy. Satan offers delights that are tantalizing. He will stimulate our passions and promise endless pleasures. But the payments he extracts are staggering!

6:13 Do not let any part of your bodies become tools of wickedness, to be used for sinning; but give yourselves completely to God — every part of you (TLB).

Each one of us decides which rules we will follow.

6:19...Ye have yielded your members servants to uncleanness...Now yield your members servants to righteousness unto holiness.

It is easy to yield our minds to uncleanness but then we become the servants of uncleanness.

Keep Moving Forward!

6:22 Now being made free from sin, and become servants to God, ye have your fruit unto holiness, and the end everlasting life.

God frees us from the eternal penalty of sin. In return for His gift, He is asking that all the fruits of our lives be holy.

8:5 They that are after the flesh do MIND the things of the flesh; but they that are after the spirit the things of the spirit. 6 for to be carnally (sensually) MINDED is death; but to be spiritually MINDED is life and peace.

The carnal mind always insists that its urges lead to delightful pleasures.

8:7 The carnal (sensual) MIND is enmity against God: for it is not subject to the law of God.

Our natural mind does not want to subject itself to the law of God. Some believe that a Christian who abstains from immoral acts is being as spiritual as anyone could be. But the Holy Spirit wants to lead us into giving our minds to God. He understands the struggle that goes on in our hearts and He knows how resistant our minds are to God's control.

8:13 If ye live after the flesh ye shall die: but if ye through the Spirit do mortify the deeds of the body ye shall live.

To "mortify" means to subdue by discipline or self-denial. If you have permitted yourself to become a person with little or no self discipline, study this verse. Spiritual weakness or even spiritual death can result from simply doing what *we want to do.*

12:1 Present your bodies a living sacrifice, holy, acceptable unto God, which is your reasonable service.

God considers holy minds a reasonable (just and fair) standard for His children.

13:9 Thou shalt not commit adultery.

The Old Testament commandment is confirmed as part of the New.

13:14 Make not provision for the flesh, to fulfill the lusts thereof.

If we deliberately look at that which encourages immoral thinking, we are "making provision" for the flesh. If we do this, of course the flesh will enjoy itself.

117

I CORINTHIANS

3:16 Know ye not that ye are the temple of God, and that the Spirit of God dwelleth in you? 17 If any man defile (makes filthy) the temple of God, him shall God destroy; for the temple of God is holy, which temple ye are.

To defile God's temple is a fearful thing! The crafty carnal mind sometimes reaches this conclusion: "There is no way that I could keep my mind from thinking brief immoral thoughts. If I *can't* keep myself from doing that, then I am not accountable."

4:5 ...the Lord will bring to light the hidden things of darkness and will make manifest the counsels of the heart.

God will one day display our secret world of the mind and heart. Will they be X-rated? R-rated? PG-rated? How about G-rated (God approved)!

6:9 Be not deceived: neither fornicators, nor idolaters, nor adulterers, nor effeminate, nor abusers of themselves with mankind. 10...shall inherit the kingdom of God.

Immorality in any form keeps us from entering into the delightful pleasures of fellowship with God.

6:20 Glorify God in your body, and in your spirit, which are God's (RSV).

Since God is Spirit, He is *especially* interested in what is happening within our spirits. If we permit ourselves to have an impure spirit, we are asking God to dwell in the midst of our uncleanness.

A woman could watch an entire football game and not be interested in anything that went on. A man might not be able to understand how she could *possibly* do this. He could give her many reasons why she should show more spirit towards such an "interesting game". But she has no "spirit for football". If you have permitted the Holy Spirit to cleanse your spirit of the desire to think immoral thoughts, another person might not be able to understand how you could have no "spirit" for such things.

10:13 There hath no temptation taken you but such as is common to man: but God is faithful, who will not suffer you to be tempted above that ye are able; but will with the temptation also make a way to escape, that ye may be able to bear it.

The temptation to think immoral thoughts is common to all men and women, but there is "a way to escape".

II CORINTHIANS

4:2 (We)...have renounced the hidden things of dishonesty.

It would be dishonest to say we respect others as Christians, if we have hidden adulterous thoughts about them.

6:14 Be ye not unequally yoked together with unbelievers.

If we should have immoral thoughts about a person who is an unbeliever, this would be union with that unbeliever. The verse goes on to describe such a union as "communion with darkness".

7:1 Let us cleanse ourselves from all filthiness of the flesh and spirit, perfecting holiness in the fear of God.

This verse is not directed at spiritual giants. It is to all who "fear God". 10:5 Casting down IMAGINATIONS... and bringing into captivity every THOUGHT to the obedience of Christ.

God says we *can* control our imaginations and thoughts! This is good news!

120

> *11:3 I fear, lest by any means, as the serpent be-guiled Eve through his subtlety, so your MINDS should be corrupted.*

Eve looked at the forbidden fruit and it *looked good.* I'm sure she didn't feel at the time that her mind was being "corrupted". Eve had never before sinned yet she was subject to being deceived by Satan. If you have ever looked at forbidden fruit and wanted it, you were being tempted by the same tempter!

GALATIANS

> *5:16 Walk in the Spirit, and ye shall not fulfill the lust of the flesh. 17 For the flesh lusteth against the Spirit, and the Spirit against the flesh: and these are contrary the one to the other: so that ye cannot do the things that ye would.*

It is extremely important to learn that the Holy Spirit is often directly opposed to what the flesh wants. The flesh can say, "But I don't see why this thing I want to do is wrong!" This is our golden opportunity to say, "I will not do what my flesh wants!"

> *5:19 Now the works of the flesh are manifest, which are these: adultery, fornication, unclean-ness.*

This verse gives us a clear picture of what the Bible means when it speaks of "the flesh".

5:24 Those who belong to Christ Jesus have put to death their human nature, with all its passions and desires. 25 The Spirit has given us life; he must also control our lives (GN).

As the Spirit controls our minds, He will give us *great joy*. And the more He controls, the greater our joy! God created us and He knows what will bring us the greatest pleasure.

There is a war going on. Our flesh demands immoral thinking. Our spirits cry out to be pure in heart. Each of us must decide where the victory will be.

EPHESIANS

2:2 We once conducted ourselves in line with the ways of this world system. 3 We indulged our fleshly desires and carried out the inclinations of our lower nature and our THOUGHTS (MLB).

If a certain thought is one that God forbids, the mind attempts to find some clever way to excuse itself. It wants to be "indulged".

4:22 Put off your old nature which belongs to your former manner of life and is corrupt through deceitful lusts."

This is something we must do after we have accepted Christ. But we need to be aware that "deceitful lusts" are exactly that — deceitful. They present themselves as being perfectly reasonable and logical.

4:23 Be renewed in the spirit of your minds (RSV).

A blessed potential, but again it is something *we* must do.

4:24 Put on the new man, which...is created in righteousness and true holiness.

Meditate for a moment on what this "new man" would be like — created *by God* to be righteous and holy. What kind of thoughts would flow through his mind?

5:3 Fornication, and all uncleanness, or covetousness, let it not be once named among you, as becometh saints. 11 Have no fellowship with the unfruitful works of darkness, but rather reprove them.

Our minds want to enjoy fellowship with uncleanness but our spirits want to reprove.

5:12 For it is a shame even to speak of those things which are done of them in secret.

Secret thoughts are often worthy of shame.

6:13 Take unto you the whole armour of God, that ye may be able to withstand in the evil day, and having done all, to stand.

It takes *all* of God's spiritual resources to withstand the temptation toward evil thoughts and desires.

Keep Learning!

PHILIPPIANS

4:8 Finally, brethren, whatsoever things are true, whatsoever things are honest...whatsoever things are pure...whatsoever things are of good report; if there be any virtue, and if there be any praise, THINK on these things.

If we act on this verse, God sends heavenly hosts to assist us. Our thoughts become tools that He can use to bless our own lives and many others.

COLOSSIANS

3:1 If ye then be risen with Christ, seek those things which are above, where Christ sitteth on the right hand of God.

What a calling! Willingly do those things, and think those thoughts that would be acceptable in God's presence!

3:2 Set your affection on things above, not on things on the earth.

If we pray, "God, change my thinking," we are asking Him to do what He has told us to do.

3:5 Put to death...evil desires and covetousness (RSV).

"But how could I possibly stop *wanting* something that I want?"

God's Word can help us accomplish this, but we must meditate on what He has said and then make a decision to change our desires.

I THESSALONIANS

4:4 God wants you to be holy and pure, and to keep clear of all sexual sin (TLB).

If we have things on our minds that are not pure, He is saying, "Keep clear!"

4:7 For God hath not called us unto uncleanness, but unto holiness.

Once we have accepted forgiveness of our sins, we then have a high calling. God's standard is, "Move toward holiness." He is always patient, but He may bring pressure to bear if we are not moving in the right direction.

II THESSALONIANS

1:11 We pray for you constantly, that God will think you worthy of this calling, and that he will effect in you all that his goodness desires to do."

God desires to build and strengthen goodness in us. If our minds are infected with unclean desires, He is thwarted in His plans. Since He has given us freedom to choose whatever we will, He accepts our decisions. We have a grand opportunity.

I TIMOTHY

4:12 Be thou an example of the believers in... purity. 15 Meditate upon these things; give thyself wholly to them.

If we, like Timothy, will meditate on God's Word, and give ourselves to it, we too can become an example "in purity".

II TIMOTHY

2:20 There are dishes made of gold and silver as well as some made from wood and clay. The expensive dishes are used for guests, and the cheap ones are used in the kitchen or to put garbage in. 21 If you stay away from sin you will be like one of these dishes made of purest gold...so that Christ himself can use you for his highest purposes (TLB).

We select the quality of our thoughts and thereby select the quality of our service to God.

To be purified, gold and silver must be placed over fire. The heat forces the impurities to the surface where they can be skimmed off. The Word of God is a purifying fire that will bring to the surface things that have no value.

2:22 Flee also youthful lusts: but follow righteousness, faith, charity, peace, with them that call on the Lord out of a pure heart.

If we cry to God, "Lord, increase my faith and love and peace," but permit uncleanliness in our hearts, our prayers may accomplish little. Understanding this will help us to see why some of our prayers have gone unanswered.

TITUS

1:15 Unto the pure all things are pure: but unto them that are defiled and unbelieving is nothing pure; but even their MIND and conscience is defiled.

A "pure" mind looks on a member of the opposite sex and has "pure" thoughts. But if our "mind and conscience" have become defiled we think impure thoughts.

1:16 They profess that they know God; but in works they deny him, being abominable, and disobedient.

It is easy to say, "I know God." But if we are disobedient, we are "denying Him".

PHILEMON

1:6 I pray that as you share your faith with others it will grip their lives too, as they see the wealth of good things in you (TLB).

As our minds are cleansed, people will see the "wealth of good things" in us.

Seeds of pure thinking were sown in our hearts when we accepted Jesus. We can cause these seeds to grow and bear much fruit.

HEBREWS

4:12 The word of God is quick, and powerful... and is a discerner of the THOUGHTS and intents of the heart.

This verse offers to us the solution to the moral and spiritual problems that I have mentioned in this book. God knows our thoughts and has provided His Word to assist us. But His words will not work in us unless we meditate on them and then make personal decisions based on what He tells us.

What would you do if you had the perfect opportunity to commit some immoral act? What you would *like* to do reflects the person you *are* and reflects the "intents" of your heart.

JAMES

1:14 A man's temptation is due to the pull of his own inward desires, which can be enormously attractive. His own desire takes hold of him and that produces sin (Phillips).

I don't ever like to blame myself!

When we are tempted, it seems ever so easy to give in. We need to look into the future and examine what *could happen* if we permit lust to live in our hearts. It is deadly, destructive and powerful.

1:22 Be ye doers of the word, and not hearers only.

Part of being a "doer" of the Word, is striving to cleanse our minds.

4:4 Ye adulterers and adulteresses, know ye not that the friendship of the world is enmity with God? Whosoever therefore will be a friend of the world is the enemy of God.

An "enemy of God"? Not an enviable position!

4:8 Purify your hearts, ye doubleminded.

This is having one mind that says, "I want to please God," and another mind that says, "I want to enjoy impure thoughts."

Keep Scriptures on Your Mind!

I PETER

*1:6 Ye are in heaviness through manifold temp-
tations.*

Yielding to the temptation of immoral thinking will bring a
sense of heaviness to any person who is seeking to do God's
will. Our conscience is alerting us that something is wrong.

*2:11 Dearly beloved, I beseech you as strangers
and pilgrims, abstain from fleshly lusts, which
war against the soul.*

Our limited comprehension of spiritual matters prevents
us from understanding how destructive lust is.

II PETER

1:5 Giving all diligence, add to your faith virtue.

All too frequently Christians are led into seeking more
faith, but are not taught to seek virtue. Peter is telling us
that we must use "all diligence" in this important matter.

*2:9 The Lord knoweth how to deliver the godly
out of temptations.*

I have learned that when a man or woman begin their efforts to have only clean thoughts on their minds, they
often feel as if the goal is impossible. The mind may say, "I
can never do what you are asking me!" At that point it is a
great joy to read God's promise that He knows how to deliver us out of temptations.

2:19...Whatever overcomes a man, to that he is enslaved (RSV).

When another person causes you to enter into lustful thoughts, that person is overcoming you. If a woman does this to a man she is literally overcoming him. He usually has no feeling of being "overcome", and would probably staunchly deny it, but in God's eyes that is what happens. If a man draws a woman into immorality by persuasive words or conduct, he is overcoming her, and she is under his bondage.

2:20 For if after they have escaped the pollutions of the world through the knowledge of the Lord and Saviour Jesus Christ, they are again entangled therein, and overcome...22 It is happened unto them according to the true proverb, The dog is turned to his own vomit.

A dog returning to its vomit is a distasteful picture. A Christian whose eyes are "full of adultery" would be equally as offensive to God.

3:14 Be diligent that ye may be...without spot, and blameless.

God is saying to us, "Be pure. Be blameless. Be holy."

I JOHN

2:6 He that saith he abideth in him ought himself also so to walk, even as he (Jesus) walked.

Such a glorious goal — to learn to have thoughts similar to Christ's!

2:16 For all that is in the world, the lust of the flesh and the lust of the eyes...is not of the Father, but is of the world.

To lust after something that does not belong to us may seem to be very natural, but that desire is "not of the Father".

3:3 Every man that hath this hope in him purifieth himself, even as he (Christ) is pure.

This is seemingly an impossible task, but it gives us a vivid picture of what God wants us to do with our minds. For many years I frequently, and I confess, quite piously prayed, "Oh God, please purify me from these bad thoughts." I finally realized that He was saying, "Merlin, you do it!"

3:21 Beloved, if our heart condemn us not then have we confidence toward God.

Our heart's ability to tell us that all is not well in our thought life is a valuable gift from God. He is helping us feel what He feels so we can make necessary changes. Then when our hearts are free of guilt we have new confidence. In my own case I recall feeling as if a great load had been lifted from my shoulders. I can easily sympathize with those who carry a burden of guilt. It is both tiring and painful.

3:22 And whatsoever we ask, we receive of him, because we keep his commandments and do those things that are pleasing in his sight.

God's promises of good things can be claimed when we do those things that are pleasing to Him!

II JOHN

1:2 For the truth's sake, which dwelleth in us, and shall be with us for ever.

It is this abiding truth, in the hearts of all Christians, that makes us feel guilty when we have wrong thoughts.

III JOHN

1:2 Beloved, I wish above all things that thou mayest prosper and be in health, even as thy soul prospereth.

It is good to be ready for our finances and health to prosper proportionately to the moral condition of our minds!

1:11 Beloved, follow not that which is evil but that which is good.

The words, "follow not" also mean, "do not imitate". Passion frequently draws us into imitating, in our minds, things that are evil.

REVELATION

3:10 Because you have patiently obeyed Me...I will protect you from the time of Great Tribulation and temptation, which will come upon the world to test everyone alive (TLB).

Involvement in immoral activity is one of the most persistent temptations facing present-day Christians. We are surrounded by every conceivable opportunity to think impure thoughts. Nearly every movie and TV program is, in one way or another, trying to convince us that immorality should not be considered an evil thing. Jesus is forewarning us of what we should expect. He is also promising us great reward if we overcome!

2:7 He that hath an ear, let him hear what the Spirit saith...To him that overcometh:

1. I give to eat of the tree of life (2:7).
2. He shall not be hurt of the second death (2:11).
3. I give to eat of the hidden manna (2:17).
4. I give a new name which no man knoweth saving he that receiveth it (2:17).
5. I give power over the nations (2:26).
6. I give the morning star (2:28).
7. He shall be clothed in white raiment (3:5).
8. I will not blot out his name out of the book of life (3:5).
9. I will confess his name before my Father, and before his angels (3:5).
10. Will I make a pillar in the temple of my God (3:12).
11. I will write upon him the name of my God (3:12).
12. I will write upon him my new name (3:12).
13. Will I grant to sit with me in my throne, even as I also overcame, and am set down with my Father in his throne (3:21).

3:22 He that hath an ear let him hear what the Spirit saith.

19:6 After that I heard what sounded like the shout of a vast throng, like the boom of many pounding waves and like the roar of terrific and mighty thunderpeals, exclaiming, Hallelujah — praise the Lord! For now the Lord our God the Omnipotent — the All-Ruler — reigns!

19.7 Let us rejoice — and shout for joy — exulting and triumphant! Let us celebrate and ascribe to Him glory and honor, for the marriage of the Lamb has come and His bride has prepared herself.

19:8 She has been permitted to dress in fine linen — dazzling and white, for the fine linen represents the righteousness — the upright, just and godly living and right standing with God (AMP).

When we adorn ourselves with pure thoughts we are putting on bridal garments, preparing for the coming of the bridegroom!

EPILOGUE

What will you do when you have completed this book? Have I given you sufficient help to bring about lasting changes in *What's on Your Mind*? These questions have been on *my* mind for many months.

Remember the man who loved hot fudge sundaes and had been told he had diabetes? You may have thought, Sure, he lost his desire for sundaes but the desire would immediately return if he found there had been a wrong diagnosis. So, his desire really hadn't changed at all — he only replaced it for a time with a stronger desire — to live.

That's the way all our natural desires are. Here is an illustration that explains what happens when we change our desires. Let's climb aboard a rocket and blast off. We go into orbit three hundred fifty miles above the earth. Our rocket is within the gravitational pull of earth but has sufficient speed to stay in its orbit. Picture two possibilities:

1. If the rocket should slow down, it would be drawn back to the earth.

2. If the rocket received a rapid forward thrust it could slip out of the earth's gravitational range and race into space.

Imagine the earth as being your *former* desire for immoral thoughts. You are now out in orbit and are in a sense free. But...you are free *because of* your forward speed. You have decided to follow God's will and your thinking has entered a new dimension, where you no longer need to be ashamed of your desires.

What influence does your old desire for immoral thoughts have over you? If you "slow down" your orbit, your rocket will be pulled back to your old desires. That's the way life is on planet earth.

What will slow our orbital speed?

1. Getting our attention off the things God has told us about thoughts, desires and imaginations.

2. Deliberately placing ourselves in a position where old desires can reassert themselves.

3. Failing to have regular fellowship with God so His Holy Spirit can hold our attention.

But what about the second alternative where our rocket is thrust into space and leaves the gravitational pull of our immoral desires? I believe this glorious time will come when our spirits slip out of these bodies and race upward to God! At that rapturous moment our impure desires are gone forever! Until then they will be an attraction to us. The good news is that we can stay in orbit and out of their control. Jesus provided the thrust to set us free.

Here is the plan:

Get into orbit if you aren't already there!

Stay in orbit!

Live where the mind is free of earth's pollution.

A SPECIAL NOTE

Once we are willing to expose our thoughts to everyone, we will be motivated to excellence in *all* our thinking.

God's desire for His children is that even the most secret thoughts of our hearts be blessed by His Spirit. To be blessed by the Spirit of God is the *highest and most rewarding* experience we can have on this earth.

THINGS YOU CAN DO IN YOUR COMMUNITY

You are surrounded by men and women who urgently need to read this book. God will abundantly bless your efforts to share its message with them.

Some of the nicest people you know may joyfully receive this message. Pastors and spiritual leaders have told me they believe that *What's on Your Mind?* can cause a moral and spiritual awakening in our land.

Obtain as many copies as you can, and then keep them circulating throughout your community. Your personal efforts can bring new spiritual life and strength to thousands. You can help to prevent heartbreaking tragedies that come to those who have not realized the importance of what is going on in their minds.

Give a copy to every minister in your community and to everyone who teaches young people.

Visit local Christian bookstores to see if they are carrying, "What's on Your Mind?". If so, tell the manager how important its message is. If not, urge him to get a supply and to tell customers about it. Contact the store several times as a follow up. Your persistence can help bring a spiritual revival.

Please consider supplying free copies to prisoners, hospital patients and servicemen. Your donation for this purpose can be sent to:

The Foundation of Praise
Box 2518
Escondido, CA 92025

You will also want to read these other best-sellers by Merlin Carothers:

PRISON TO PRAISE

Merlin Carothers' first book. This book has been printed in thirty-one languages and distributed in over sixty countries. Many people have reported transformed lives as a result of reading the powerful message found in this book.

POWER IN PRAISE

An in-depth study of the working and scriptural basis for the principle introduced in *Prison to Praise:* in all things give praise and thanks to God. Praising God in one's predicaments is first acknowledging that God is in control of everything, whether or not it is in His will, and that He has the power to turn all things to good. Secondly, the act of obediently praising God begins to soften our hearts and produces a right heart attitude — a prerequisite for any act of God.

ANSWERS TO PRAISE

The proof of the pudding! No sooner did the first two Praise Books come out than the phone calls and letters started pouring in. Praise works! Over-joyed Christians felt compelled to share the "signs and wonders following" with the author, adding their own testimonies to the rapidly-growing record. Miracle upon miracle, from all walks of life!

PRAISE WORKS

More letters selected from an assortment of thousands illustrate the secret of *freedom through praise!* Includes a letter from Frank Foglio — (author of *Hey, God!*) — who learned the power of praise when his daughter recovered miraculously after 7 long years in the "hopeless" ward of an institution for the mentally ill. Other letters are from a nurse, a nun, an attorney, a blind girl, a chaplain, an alcoholic and many others! Praise for brain surgery, praise for prison, praise for the Lord!

WALKING AND LEAPING

When Merlin Carothers lost a new car and trailer, along with his most-prized possessions, in a freak traffic accident — he praised God. But when he found himself singlehandedly overseeing the construction of a massive church building with only the enthusiastic but unskilled labor of his parishioners, and with the precarious backing of a bank balance that generally registered zero, he had to learn to "praise God in all things" all over again. "Fascinating and exciting. I thoroughly enjoyed it." — New Life Magazine

BRINGING HEAVEN INTO HELL

Now Merlin Carothers goes beyond his earlier works to explore life-changing situations which others have experienced. The author shares these discoveries of God's forgiveness, a new freedom in Christ and the power of the Holy Spirit to shed light from heaven in the midst of a personal hell.

VICTORY ON PRAISE MOUNTAIN

When Merlin Carothers met with contention and dissension in his church, he learned to apply in his own life the principles he has taught to millions of others. This intensely personal account shows how genuine, spontaneous praise often leads into valleys that are direct paths to higher ground.

THE BIBLE ON PRAISE

This beautifully-printed, four-color, thirty-two page booklet features selected verses on praise from thirty-eight books of the Bible. These are Merlin's favorite verses and were personally selected by him. This booklet makes a lovely gift with a message that will bless the reader for years.

MORE POWER TO YOU

Worldwide demand for more information on power has resulted in *More Power To You* — written for persons in everyday places who need more power in their everyday lives. Though presented in simple easy-to-read language, the author has given us profound and useful insights into serious problems of modern life. This book is a beautiful key to unlock a vast storehouse of spiritual power.

ALSO AVAILABLE ON CASSETTE:

Prison to Praise Album
 (set of 6 teaching tapes) $24.95
Power in Praise Album
 (set of 6 teaching tapes) $24.95
Individual Tapes
How God Taught Me $4.95
How to Receive the Baptism
 in the Holy Spirit $4.95
How Not to be Irritated $4.95
Created to Believe $4.95
The Excitement of Praising God $4.95
Your Greatest Miracle $4.95
Roots of Bitterness $4.95

If this book has been a blessing to you, please let me know. Each month I prepare *Praise News* in which I share new things that I learn about praise. I will be pleased to send this to you at no charge if you request it.

Comments, inquiries, requests for speaking engagements, recorded messages and sermons, prison, hospital and military ministries, other books and prayer requests should be directed to:

Merlin R. Carothers
Box 2518
Escondido, CA 92025